JOHN
SLIDELL

John Slidell, circa 1864. After a drawing from a daguerreotype
by Thomas Slidell.

JOHN SLIDELL
AND THE CONFEDERATES
IN PARIS (1862-65)

....

BY BECKLES WILLSON

AMS PRESS
NEW YORK

Reprinted from the edition of 1932, New York
First AMS EDITION published 1970
Manufactured in the United States of America

Library of Congress Catalog Card Number: 77-111089
SBN: 404-06992-4

AMS PRESS, INC.
New York, N.Y. 10003

To my Friends of l'Ile St. Louis,
KATHLEEN AND TUDOR WILKINSON

CONTENTS

ILLUSTRATIONS

FOREWORD

I⊤ has always appeared to me a serious omission on the part of the historians of the American Confederacy to have left untouched, or touched upon so slightly, the ceaseless activities of the able agents, emissaries and champions, paid and unpaid, of the Lost Cause in Europe. In the ensuing chapters, I have sought to remedy this neglect. I have presented the salient facts of these activities in so far as they concern Slidell and France as I have gleaned them from every source made available to me.

At the outset I wish gratefully to acknowledge what a real boon the American Library in Paris and the Franco-American collection of the late H. C. Wallace, now at the American Embassy, have shown themselves to be.

Amongst my authorities, Professor Sears's excellent monograph on Slidell, although instructive about his subject's character and political career in America, contains only a few pages about the Paris Commissionership. It is unfortunate that the mass of official correspondence which accumulated at the Confederate office in the rue Marignan, was destroyed by Slidell himself about the year 1866, for fear of compromising the authors; but there still exists in Washington the Slidell-Benjamin correspondence, the Slidell-Mason correspondence, and other valuable letters and papers. I have also made use of various letters and memoranda belonging to the Eustis family, as well as other material compiled by the late Henri Vignaud. I have availed myself freely of the Memoirs of Captain J. D. Bulloch and other naval officers and, most of all, of Consul-General (afterwards Minister) John Bigelow's three portly volumes dealing with his Paris consular and diplomatic experiences. I have also consulted the newspapers and pamphlets of the period. On the whole, then, I feel that my pages convey a fair idea of the protracted arguments, efforts and intrigues, directed by a man of ability and experience, to obtain official recognition for his country from the Emperor, Napoleon III, as well as to promote the naval and other interests of the Confederacy in France.

During a long residence in Paris I have conversed, from time to time, with many of those who knew personally the actors in that restless drama, and count amongst my friends today some of their descendants and relations. All this has served to stimulate a natural interest; for as a Canadian I could not forget our contemporary sympathy for those of the South whom Secretary Seward delighted to call "traitors," "insurgents" and "pirates," but in whom we could only recognise patriots battling for independence.

If there is a moral in the story, it is the fatal price the South had to pay for its leaders' insistence upon the tenet of slavery, which although never seriously discussed with Slidell by Napoleon, really made recognition by both England and France impossible.

I tender here my special thanks to Madame Marchand, Slidell's granddaughter, for the portrait of Mrs. Slidell: to Baron Emile d'Erlanger for that of his mother (Matilda Slidell) and to Mr. Thomas Slidell for the drawing he has kindly made from a daguerreotype of his distinguished relative.

B. W.

Paris,
July 1st, 1932.

JOHN
SLIDELL

☆

CHAPTER I

THE "TRENT" AFFAIR

THE gangplanks of the steamer were drawn up. A group of distinguished passengers who had been waiting for three weeks at Havana for the passage to England were at last safely on board. Night drew on, a tropic night, sultry, luminous, heavy with scent; the steamer ploughed her way confidently through the waters, and the party of travellers, heaving a sigh of relief that after so many vicissitudes they were now on their way to safety and Europe, sought, one by one, their cabins. The captain had retired; even the courtly British naval officer in charge of her Britannic Majesty's mails, who had interrupted his reading of *Essays and Reviews* to lavish attentions upon the ladies of the party, now returned to his literary and theological ecstasies. All was silent save for the clank of the engines and the muffled churning of the ship's propeller.

But there was one passenger, the most notable of

those who had joined the steamer at Havana, who, unable to sleep, re-emerged at a late hour to pace the deck alone. He was an old man, though active and erect, with long grey hair. His features were ruddy and well-cut and his grey eye was piercing as a falcon's. An old man who had led an adventurous life since the day he had winged his man in a duel in his native New York nearly fifty years ago and decamped to New Orleans; a life of legal chicanery and political intrigue, of a struggle, often sordid, for wealth, place and power. His mind went back now to his gradual rise in worldly fortune, his seat in Congress, the important mission to Mexico, his election as United States Senator, his grimly-fought battles with rivals and enemies. And then—then had come the cataclysm.

Never, never had he thought to have lived to be engaged in such a tremendous adventure as this. He had thought a cataclysm might come, but not in his time. With what swiftness the shuttle of Fate had moved! A hurried decision on the part of a handful of desperate men, a cannon-shot fired at Charleston and a great nation sundered in twain. Well, history was repeating itself. Once again a group of American Colonies had declared their independence and set up a second republic alongside the first. Already much blood had been spilt; the South had met its enemies on the battlefield and routed them. But its ports were blockaded; ships, armaments and stores were lacking and it looked across the Atlantic to Europe for recognition and succour, even as the original Thirteen Colonies had done in 1776.

And so the Confederacy had chosen its emissaries, and this old man, with the long hair, steely eye and rather pompous manner, was bound for France as the envoy and representative of his country, even as the illustrious Benjamin Franklin had been some eighty-odd years before. To France, the land of his wife's ancestors, the motherland of so many of the Louisiana population, whose tongue he now spoke with tempered fluency, whose legal code he had professionally expounded, whose literature, institutions and manners he professed to admire more than those of the English. If there, with that monarch, court and people, he could succeed as Franklin had succeeded, if he could obtain recognition and support for his country, what triumph would be his! With such an ally, the cause of the Confederacy would be won. What a glorious climax to a career which, in spite of wealth and occasional office, was, somehow, a disappointment. For he knew that he was not beloved, that his character and his words were not everywhere respected; that he was charged with venality, arrogance, vindictiveness.

But if he prevailed, he felt he would go down in history as a patriot and a hero.

Even Franklin had had his enemies and his detractors—before 1777.

He had no confidence in England nor in any efforts to change English policy towards his country, in spite of all that was said and hoped to the contrary. It was to France and her all-powerful Emperor that the Confederacy must turn in its need. Napoleon III was not as English statesmen were, helpless in the hands of a canting, humanitarian democracy; once he was convinced of the expediency of intervention he could and would act. His whole career was a demonstration of this.

Thus pacing the steamer's deck, his mind busy with the problems and the diplomatic programme before him, the old man heard a step behind him and a voice addressed him by name.

"Good evening, Mr. Slidell!"

It was the burly and affable British naval officer, Commander Williams. He explained that he had been so completely absorbed in a new book which had reached him at Havana that the hours had slipped by and the striking of eight bells had startled him. "You should read it, sir—a most remarkable work. It has created an enormous sensation at home." But the distinguished passenger was not, it appeared, interested in Anglican theology.

"What lights are those?" he asked, pointing to the shore.

"We are just off Cardenas. Now, if we could steam ahead at this rate we should be in Plymouth by the 25th." There was a pause and then the officer said, "Mr. Slidell, it may interest you to know that twenty years ago I knew your brother Alexander, captain of the *Somers.*"

Had it not been so dark he would have seen that his companion's face instantly lost its ruddy hue. He always paled at the mention of his dead brother; was always unnerved. Now, he stopped in his walk and gripped the taffrail.

"My brother—Alec—you knew him?"

"We often met. The first time was at Canton in '39, when I was a sub-lieutenant on the *Theseus* and again in Sydney the following year. The last time was in Liverpool a few months after—after his trial. It had left its mark—he was a changed man. A dreadful affair that."

The other returned no answer; they walked in silence a few moments and then reaching a companionway, the older man disappeared.

That such an encounter should have disconcerted

him a little was perhaps natural. Was it not singular
that on this ship which was fast carrying him into a
new life and a brighter atmosphere, there should be
one who knew his ill-fated brother, who bore another
name and whom the world at large had forgotten; the
naval officer against whom a number of his crew had
mutinied, who had hanged at the yard-arm, without
trial, three of the mutineers, one the son of a Cabinet
Minister, for which deed he had afterwards to face his
accusers. The whole world had once rung with the
tragedy of the *Somers* and the man of whom Fenimore
Cooper had written that "his obliquity of intellect was
such that no analysis of his motives can be made on
any consistent principle of human action"—this man
was John Slidell's own brother, who after a few years
of Ishmael-like existence had dropped down dead one
day from his horse. A gloomy man, prone to fits of
passion: in his grave these many years, but never recalled without unhappy emotion. And this Englishman, bursting out of the darkness had abruptly recalled him. Was there some omen in this?

JOHN SLIDELL first drew breath in 1793, the Year of
the Terror in France, when another New Yorker,
Gouverneur Morris, was fulfilling his dangerous mission in that country. The elder Slidell, also named

John, was a prosperous ship's chandler on Lower Broadway, in close touch with the shipmasters and seafaring men of what since the Revolution had become the busiest port in America. He had begun as a "soap-boiler and chandler" and, marrying a Scotswoman of good family named Mackenzie, the pair were eventually blessed with four sons and six daughters. John Slidell, senior, within a few years became prominent in mercantile and financial circles, was President of the Mechanics' Bank and also of the Tradesmen's Insurance Company. With the social rise of his family it was too much to expect that the paternal antecedents would be altogether forgotten. A venerable New York lady, Mrs. Gouverneur, used to relate that young John Slidell once attended a fashionable dinner party, where he made a tactless speech to his fair table companion, who turned upon him with, "Sir, *you* have been *dipped,* not *moulded* into society!" On a later occasion, when Slidell had returned from a foreign trip, a malicious voice was heard to enquire blandly if he had visited Greece.

"No; why do you ask?" asked the unsuspecting victim.

"Oh, I thought it would be natural for you to renew early association." *

* Mrs. Marian Gouverneur: *As I remember.*

But, after all, was not John Keats taunted with the apothecary's shop and must not the thrusting sons of small tradesmen expect to be twitted with their humble beginnings? Inasmuch as soap-boiling and tallow-chandlery have since won and maintained peerages, it must be said that the reproach has today rather lost its point. Young Slidell, after attending two or three terms at Columbia College, eventually joined his father in the business. As to the latter, the long years of the Embargo, followed by the disastrous War of 1812, had sadly diminished profits so that when in his early twenties John Slidell, junior, entered into partnership, the firm's bankruptcy was imminent. His father retired, but the young man was unable to avert disaster.

> "I remember him," wrote a very old lady in Paris half a century later, "as a goodlooking, fresh-faced, auburn-haired young man, very quick-tempered and of a restless disposition. One day he disappeared; we were told that he had sold out his business and gone to New Orleans. And we never saw him again."

The immediate cause of Slidell's abrupt departure was his duel with Stephen Price, manager of the Park Theatre, concerning a female member of the company. Having wounded his opponent, he fled to escape arrest. Difficulties with his creditors may also have influenced his decision which had doubtless long been meditated. For youthful migration from the East had already begun in America, the West and South offering dazzling opportunities to men of energy and enterprise. Several of Slidell's companions had gone forth to take up lands or practise their callings on the Ohio and the Mississippi. One brilliant New Yorker, a friend of his father, who had likewise got into serious financial difficulties, had settled in New Orleans and had prospered there, marrying a Creole lady and becoming a distinguished jurist. This was Edward Livingston, afterwards Minister to France. His example fired young Slidell; he, too, would go to New Orleans; he, too, would become a lawyer; perhaps in time he, too, would marry a Creole lady, rise to be a distinguished jurist and even be sent by his countrymen as envoy to France. In fact, all these things eventually happened, a striking instance of the deliberate pursuit and completion of a biographical parallel.

In considering John Slidell and his future career, it is worth noting that the generality of the Northerners who went to dwell in the South became at last, as was said of the English in Ireland, more native than the natives themselves. The character, as well as the environment, of the slave-owning class differed singu-

larly from the character and environment of the upper
and middle classes of the Northern States. Those of the
latter who settled in the South gradually developed
quite un-Northern traits and adopted a different social
tone. They became more arrogant, more intense, more
passionate, and yet more ceremonious in their daily
relationships; and although perhaps not fuller of
prejudices, yet their prejudices were of a wholly contrary sort. Also their native humour, the birthright of
the true Yankee, entirely disappeared.

When John Slidell arrived in the Louisiana metropolis in 1819 and had respectfully waited upon Mr.
Livingston and several of his father's old friends, acquaintances and customers, he resolutely set about the
study of law. To this end, he accepted a clerkship in
the office of a New Orleans marine store-keeper,
spending his nights poring over text-books on Roman
law, mercantile contracts, marine law and the Code
Napoleon. Once admitted to the Louisiana bar he soon
got a footing on the ladder. Thereafter, his ascent was
rapid.

In 1828, at the age of thirty-five, he stood for Congress as a supporter of Andrew Jackson and, although
defeated, managed to get himself appointed to a local
office, until his opponents ejected him. By 1822 Slidell
was a notable political wire-puller. He boasted that

John Slidell at the age of thirty

he was making $10,000 a year at the bar and that noth-
ing the Government had to offer would induce him
to abandon it. "But," wrote Secretary of State Van
Buren to the President, after a chat in Washington
with Slidell, "he would not conceal from me that
the offer of any place of sufficient respectability
—such as a Chargé's—would be grateful to his feelings."

The secret cause of this sudden diplomatic aspira-
tion was that his friend and patron, Livingston, had
just been appointed to France as American Minister.
Livingston told Slidell that he only intended to remain
eighteen months in Paris. But Livingston's daughter's
marriage brought about a change in his official house-
hold; he decided to take his son-in-law, Barton, with
him as Secretary of Legation and so Slidell's hope of
being Chargé d'Affaires in Paris vanished.

Moreover, the good will of the President and Van
Buren did not last. "Knowing," wrote "Old Hickory"
from the White House at Washington, "that you had
a favourable oppinion of mr. Slidel [sic] as well as
myself this letter is written to put you on your guard
of this man, that you may not break your shins over
stools not in your way, and that you may be guarded
in any communications you may happen to make with
him."

The meaning of this, although awkward in orthography and expression, is plain enough and hardly complimentary to the rising politician from Louisiana. Concealing his chagrin at the coldness of the Administration towards him, Slidell, in 1834, proposed himself to the local legislature as a candidate for the United States Senate. Although his public offer was rejected, a private one in another quarter was crowned with success. A young lady of Creole family, Marie Mathilde Deslonde, consented to become his wife. She was the daughter of a French officer and was only twenty, less than half the age of the bridegroom, who, nevertheless, as we shall see, after a long and happy marriage, survived her.

It was about this time, too, that a young Jewish law student, whose parents were refugees from the British West Indies, entered his office as clerk. The name of this young man was Judah Philip Benjamin, and a few years later he was taken into partnership.

The later career of Benjamin, as United States Senator, Secretary of State to the Confederacy, and (after the war) British jurist and King's Counsel, for variety of vicissitude and continuous success until his death in Paris in 1884, is perhaps without parallel in legal or other annals.

Slidell was a member of Congress in 1845 when the

relations of the United States with Mexico were becoming insufferable to both sides. The expansionists,
filibusters and slavery men were determined not only
to annex Texas, but to run the American boundary
line down to the Rio Grande. The American Government already had a little bill against Mexico for various alleged crimes, debts and misdemeanours, and
Mexico, on her part, hated "los Americanos" with an
authentic Spanish hatred, mixed with native Mexican
venom, for their insults, violence and arrogance. President Polk, wishing to avert war if possible, thought
that Mexico might be placated on a cash basis, by
means of the venal group of political adventurers then
in power. His Secretary of State, Buchanan, made overtures, and at last the ruling junta agreed to receive an
American envoy, one "commissioned with full power
to settle the dispute in a peaceful, reasonable and honourable manner." It was a thoroughly Utopian idea:
and the expansionists and filibusters must have laughed
in derision; but it sounded well.

Buchanan offered the mission to Slidell. The latter
thought the post promised to be "at least a responsible
one and should a negotiation be brought to a favourable issue, credit and reputation will be acquired. I
think I ought not to decline."

This was Slidell's mistake. He was ignorant of the

real situation. He ought to have declined or at least have stipulated that he would not proceed to his post until preliminaries had been firmly settled and the Mexican people had confirmed the promise to receive him. Albeit, he resigned his seat in Congress and set off to meet the whole swarthy tribe of political desperadoes, bandits and priests on the other side of the border, carrying in his valise the most impossible programme ever carried by any envoy. He had not only to justify the annexation of Texas to the indignant Mexicans but also to the large party in the anti-slavery States, who were bitterly hostile to the whole shady Mexican business, and to the representatives of the English and French Governments who were shocked at its cynical iniquity and almost ready—but not quite —to help the Mexicans. Considering all the circumstances, the avowed aims of the Southern States, local public opinion, and the utter intransigence of the priests and fanatics who terrorised the Mexican politicians, themselves incredibly corrupt, the best way would have abandoned pretence and *finesse* and pronounced boldly for wholesale and unmitigated annexation, as a "necessary military measure" in order to circumvent British and French designs; to have issued an ultimatum to Mexico and marched an army to her frontiers. For this is what it came to in the end, as every one who knew the country had foretold that it would.

Unhappily, Slidell went about his mission thickly shrouded in secrecy. Its precise objects were not defined, but it was rumoured throughout the Mexican provinces that not only was Texas to be given up by the ruling Junta, but that New Mexico and California were to be bartered away in exchange for twenty-five million Yankee dollars. Suspicions were aroused; the priests incited the people to fury; and the politicians dared not avow their secret proceedings. Slidell's persuasive eloquence was wasted: the emissary from Louisiana was refused any entrance at all into the country. In his utter discomfiture he at last wrote Buchanan that "further negotiations were useless until the Mexicans were convinced by a hostile demonstration that our differences must be settled promptly, either by negotiation (i.e. cash) or the sword."

With this threat Slidell withdrew to Jalapa to await events, and there he remained until President Polk at last let loose his dogs of war upon the distracted Mexicans, whose forts were demolished, their capital occupied and vast new territories, fertile and auriferous, added to the triumphant northern Republic.

On Slidell's return from his Mexican mission, where military victory had saved his face, he proceeded to attach himself to the rising political fortunes of James Buchanan and to aim at the control of the Democratic party machine in his State. He was so far successful that a few years later, after he became Senator, the chief New Orleans newspaper could allege: "Here in Louisiana Slidellians fill almost every office, at least all the chief high places."

Slidell even contrived to get his law partner, Benjamin, chosen as his colleague in the Senate. Incidentally, he built up a considerable fortune, largely in real estate, by methods which, if his enemies are to be believed, were not always above suspicion.

When Buchanan, largely through Slidell's efforts, became President in 1857, he offered the mission to France to Slidell, who refused it on the grounds of his preoccupation with Louisiana affairs. But this did not prevent his being one of the chief movers in a scheme for the acquisition of Cuba and in 1859 he introduced a bill in the Senate to buy that island from Spain for $30,000,000. Spain, France and England opposed the scheme and it failed to win support in the Senate. A year later Slidell changed his mind about the Paris legation and was ready to accept it in the hope of reconciling Napoleon III to the Cuban purchase. Buchanan, however, having appointed another Southerner to the post, felt a reluctance about recalling him unless, as he hastened to add, his dear friend Slidell insisted. Slidell magnanimously did not insist. But he was already beginning to feel coldly towards Buchanan.

We get a striking pen-picture of the Senator from Louisiana at the Democratic National Convention at Charleston in 1860 as he appeared to a famous American journalist, Murat Halstead:

> "Seated at a round table, on which books, newspapers and writing material are scattered about, is a gentleman with long, thin white hair, through which the top of his head blushes like the shell of a boiled lobster. The gentleman has also a cherry-red face, the color being that produced by good health, and good living joined to a florid temperament. His features are well cut, and the expression is that of a thoughtful, hard working, resolute man of the world. He is a New Yorker by birth, but has made a princely fortune at the New Orleans bar. He is not a very eloquent man in the Senate, but his ability is unquestioned; and it is universally known that he is with the present Administration, the power behind the throne greater than the throne itself. Mr. Buchanan is as wax in his fingers."

When Secession was decided upon Slidell did not hesitate a moment, but cast in his lot with the South. He had already said in Congress in 1858:

"We have every reason, so far as material interests are concerned, to be united and harmonious, but we cannot shut our eyes to the melancholy fact that at this day there prevails between the masses of the people of the Eastern and Southern States as deep a feeling of alienation—I might say of animosity—as ever existed between England and France."

When the Provisional Government of the Confederacy assembled at Montgomery, Alabama, it despatched three Commissioners to Europe, W. L. Yancey, A. Dudley Mann (of whom we shall later hear a good deal) and Peter Rost. The labours abroad of these men had not been very successful: their utterances, especially in England, had been rather tactless. It was felt that a more direct and satisfactory relationship with England and France was desirable.

In the late summer of 1861, therefore, President Jefferson Davis signed the credentials of James Murray Mason of Virginia and John Slidell of Louisiana as resident Commissioners from the Confederate States in London and Paris, respectively. Mason was the grandson of the George Mason who had signed the Declaration of Independence. He was an elderly man of mediocre ability and unattractive personality. In September the two men met in Charleston and even-

tually both found themselves passengers on board the
Trent at Havana.

On the morning following the embarkation of the two
Confederate Commissioners, November 8, 1861, John
Slidell slept until a late hour, only reappearing
amidst the company when all were assembled for
luncheon in the dining-saloon of the *Trent.* There,
noticeably graver and more distant than usual, he
joined his eminent friend and diplomatic colleague,
Mason, who sat opposite him at the captain's table.
The little party consisted of Mrs. Slidell, a comely,
rather portly brunette, with charming manners,
their two lively daughters, Matilda and Rosina, and
their son Alfred. Besides there were Slidell's secretary,
George Eustis, and his bride, a daughter of Corcoran,
the Washington banker (just now unhappily a pris-
oner in Fort Lafayette) and Mason's secretary, McFar-
land. The conversation naturally ran on their late
travelling vicissitudes, for they had gone overland
from New Orleans to Charleston and from thence to
Nassau. It had been an exciting two months' experience trying to ensure a safe passage with all these
Federal cruisers blockading the ports. The sympathetic captain assured the ladies that their anxieties
were now over and pointing gaily to the square of

bunting which was suspended beneath the Royal arms in the saloon, he said, with a little bow to Mrs. Slidell:

"The Union Jack, ladies. A good thing aboard a neutral ship: it covers the cargo—no matter how precious!"

This little gallantry was smilingly acknowledged.

The meal had scarce concluded when, through the open port-hole, the report of a cannon-shot electrified the company. They were still, in spite of the captain's gay assurances, a little nervous. Looking out upon the waters the spectators perceived a strange frigate, resting motionless a little ahead on their port bow. As they looked, an American ensign was run up from the frigate's masthead. This was serious: Captain Moir got up and went on deck. There he encountered Commander Williams, R.N., who represented the British Admiralty and was in charge of the mails. The mate reported that the stranger had fired a shot.

"Shall we slow down, sir?" he asked.

"Slow down? D—— their impudence!" cried Williams. "My advice to you, Captain, is to keep full steam ahead and show your ensign!"

The captain hardly needed this counsel: but as his ship drew nearly level to the stationary frigate another shot came hurtling through the air and exploded across his bows. Against this argument there was no evasion;

the captain ordered his engines reversed. "Keep all the passengers below," he told the mate. Already a boat was putting out from the frigate; in ten minutes more a young officer, announcing himself as Lieutenant Fairfax of the United States frigate *San Jacinto*, was standing on the deck of the *Trent*.

"I must ask you, Captain, to furnish me with your list of passengers."

"Sir," answered Captain Moir, "this is a British ship, the Royal Mail steamer *Trent*, carrying her Majesty's mails and civilian. passengers. I deny your right to make any such demand."

Fairfax then took a paper from his pocket and called out the names of four persons, the Confederate Commissioners and their secretaries, "known to be on board this ship." His orders were to bring them away at all hazards. Moir's response was:

"I refuse absolutely to give them up, or to recognise your authority to interfere with a British ship or any of its passengers."

"Very well," responded the American, "then I must take forcible possession." Observing his signal, three boatloads of American marines and sailors, numbering about ninety in all, promptly put off from the *San Jacinto*. They arrived: a rather distressing scene ensued, in which weeping women and rough seamen with drawn swords and revolvers figured. But ere this point was reached the principals, Slidell and Mason, recognised that, as far as they were concerned, the game was up and for the present their voyage and their mission to Europe were both suspended. They had already confided their despatches to the trusty purser and packed their hand baggage. They now stood by, pale but composed, with their women folk beside them.

Slidell's mind had already grasped the tremendous possibilities of the situation. In a flash he realized that the forcible seizure of civilian passengers from a British ship was an incident of international magnitude. It is true, British warships had been doing this sort of thing to neutral vessels for the best part of a century: but that was quite irrelevant. This "affront" to the British flag would have to be instantly disavowed by the Washington Government or it must accept the consequences. If Lincoln and Seward refused both surrender and apology, there was a pleasing chance that the British fleet would be bombarding Boston and New York within a month. The South would thus gain her independence without another blow being struck.

On the other hand, one could not exclude the disturbing possibility that he and Mason might be

lynched by an unruly Northern mob on their way to
a Northern prison. Slidell, like many men of violent
speech, shrank in horror from physical violence. His
knees trembled, as he embraced his wife, muttering:
"Don't be afraid, my dear; they will pay dearly for
this!"

An impatient subaltern laid a hand on his shoulder, whereat his daughter, Matilda, who was a girl of
spirit, promptly slapped the young man's face. In a
flash she had recognised the offender: she had actually danced with him the previous spring when he had
gone ashore from his ship at New Orleans. But her
action shocked the marines. With fixed bayonets up-
raised they involuntarily advanced a step towards her.
It was then that the white-haired veteran, Commander
Williams, interposed, exclaiming dramatically:

"Back, you d—d cowardly poltroons!"

It was a fine gesture, worthy of the best traditions
of seamanship and Transpontine melodrama, and the
whole scene lost nothing in the telling when recounted
later in the drawing-rooms and at the dinner-tables
of London and Paris.

Painfully the arrested diplomats and their secretaries
descended the rope-ladder into the *San Jacinto's*
boats. Lieutenant Fairfax, acting on the instructions
of his superior officer, Captain Wilkes, ordered Cap-

tain Moir himself to join them, but this the latter
indignantly refused to do and the American officer
did not persist. As for the ladies of the party, it was
hastily arranged that they should continue their voyage on the *Trent,* as far as St. Thomas.

For the ensuing half hour a quartette of distraught
women, sympathetically succoured and supported by
the entire ship's company, leant over the *Trent's* taffrail. There with pallid cheeks and streaming eyes they
continued to wave scarves and handkerchiefs towards
the diminishing hull of the *San Jacinto* until it appeared only a faint speck on the western horizon.
What terrible fate awaited their father and their husbands? And there was poor, kind old Mr. Mason
whose face had gone so grey under the ordeal, and who
was known to have a weak heart. When and where, if
ever, would the party, so brusquely, brutally sundered,
meet again?

Weeks of agonising suspense elapsed before any answer to these questions could reach them.

CHAPTER II

THE PARIS SCENE IN THE SIXTIES

THE news of the high-handed seizure of the two Confederate Commissioners astonished Europe, which had been disappointed of late in the quality of its American sensations. An unprecedented "outrage" had been committed upon the British flag on the high seas and there was not a council-chamber, chancellery, club or dinner-table where the event was not the theme of excited discussion. The names of Mason and Slidell were on every lip. It occurred to nobody to dissociate the pair. It was always Mason and Slidell (as in England) or Slidell and Mason (as in France); no one distinguished one from the other or knew anything of their character and antecedents: they were the twin victims of Yankee arrogance, the twin portents of international disaster.

Lord Lyons, the British Minister, had telegraphed the news from Washington, but it was not until the

29th of November and the arrival of the *Trent* at Plymouth that the British Cabinet was summoned to consider whether war between England and the United States was not imminent. It soon appeared that the sole initiative and responsibility for the seizure rested with Captain Charles Wilkes, commander of the *San Jacinto,* but that the Government, press and people of the Northern States gave his action the most jubilant approval. In John Slidell's words to the French Emperor, "The commander of the *San Jacinto* had been fêted wherever he went, as a conqueror; his journey from his landing at Boston to his arrival at Washington was one continual ovation; the Secretary of the Navy officially endorsed his action; the House of Representatives voted him a sword by acclamation; the President and his cabinet openly declared that the prisoners should never be surrendered and the entire press without exception denounced as cowards and traitors all who ventured even to hint that the seizure was illegal." *

On reaching Boston the four prisoners were confined in Fort Warren, all four in a single small room which served as bedroom, salon and dining-room. Yet they were not unhappy, even at the prospect of long detention, as soon as its implications were realised.

* Letter to Benjamin, July 20, 1862.

"If we are not given up, a war with England is inevitable," wrote Slidell, "and such a war is bound to be brief, in my opinion."

The *Trent* affair belongs to history. It is not only known to every American schoolboy, but to every diplomatist, every maritime lawyer, every journalist and even every legislator, however scanty his reading. The Confederate Commissioners were given up at last, in response to a tempered demand by the British Government, backed by a despatch from the French Emperor, and less than two months later their interrupted voyage to Europe was resumed. On January 30th both landed at Southampton.

Now, it is precisely at this point that the story of Mason and Slidell should advance in glowing, triumphant crescendo. They have set whole nations by the ears; they have excited the passions of men, evoked commiseration, aroused the wildest enthusiasm. Torrents of ink and forensic eloquence have been poured out in their honour. This is their last public appearance together. They had successfully escaped from the clutches of their captors. Surely, their greeting on English soil should be commensurate with the international celebrity they had enjoyed.

And indeed there had been talk of a national welcome to these whom the *Morning Post* styled "the

Heroes of the *Trent.*" But truth to tell they arrived too late. Their coming was now an anti-climax. There was a reaction in public opinion and already the *Times* had attacked them. In a leading article it recommended the British public not to make any demonstration in honour of Messrs. Mason and Slidell when they arrived. It reminded its readers that both men had gained fortune and popularity by attacking England and English policy in the past. "They need not thank this country for their liberation: it was simply a point of honour with us. It has cost us a million pounds sterling, but we would have done the same for two negro slaves." The newspaper went on to say that it could not prevent lionising; but that Tom Sayers, the pugilist, would prove just as great an attraction as Mason and Slidell, who, however, "though less beautiful than Blondin, might be an equal draw at the Crystal Palace."

"These insults from the great English journal," wrote Slidell, "stung me to the quick and I longed to make a suitable rejoinder. But it was not my place to address the English people in any way unless called upon to do so. That was Mr. Mason's province." *

Yet there were many Confederate sympathisers in England who felt that something should be done and

* Letter to H. Vignaud, April 2, 1868.

James Murray Mason
(Drawn from a daguerreotype)

had approached two of the men who had hitherto been acting as official emissaries of the Confederacy. But these men, the Hon. W. L. Yancey and Colonel A. Dudley Mann, were disappointed and disillusioned; they were besides filled with resentment at being superseded. Yancey did, however, suggest that, while a public declaration might be inexpedient, a gracefully-worded apology for having put the British Government to so much trouble might be well received. But the shock of his arrest and confinement had affected Mason: his was no bold, adventurous spirit at any time: and now, more than ever, he distrusted his powers. And so these two American statesmen, ex-Senators, distinguished jurists, representing the new Republic of the West which had just emerged into national life, crept almost shamefacedly into London, silent, unregarded by the populace, obscure.

When the United States Minister, Charles Francis Adams (grandson of the envoy whom George III and his Court had so cold-shouldered), heard that the "rebel" Commissioners had been two days in London without any popular demonstration and that Slidell was off to Paris, he smiled a sardonic smile.

"Well, there he'll find a man of his own sort who'll be delighted to see him."

The man he thus referred to was his Majesty the Emperor of the French.

To any one who, free from political or national bias, studies honestly the character of Louis Napoleon Bonaparte, the conclusion is somewhat different from that reached by some of his most notable contemporaries. It also differs from the summary and meretricious estimates of the recent school of historical *feuilletonistes* who have established the principle that not merely virtue and decency, but any personal merit, industry and unselfishness whatever attributed to a famous historical character is (to use the current phrase) "bunk."

Judged fairly, Napoleon III was not only the bearer of a splendid name, but was in himself a remarkable man. His intellectual powers were considerable; they had been fortified by much reading and reflection; he was a shrewd judge of most men and women; he was animated by a genuine desire to benefit humanity, to increase the wealth, prestige and happiness of all Frenchmen, and to dwell on terms of peace, if possible, with his neighbours. It is of no use to heap up evidence against him, tending to disprove this view of his character, to exhibit him as intellectually mediocre, false, mean-spirited—sensual, cynical, superstitious and ambitious; an inveterate *intriguant,* hypocrite and moral coward. We may leave this sort of violent abuse to Victor Hugo, Henri Rochefort and the race of severe and uncompromising political doctrinaires who still profess themselves horrified not only at Louis Napoleon's Coup d'Etat of 1851 but by Benito Mussolini's Coup d'Etat in 1922, forgetting that when the overturning of any constitutional régime is approved by the people and is beneficial to the country, it cannot be a "crime." If it is not criminal for the many to throw off allegiance to one man, it is not criminal for one man to throw off allegiance to the many, assuming his motives to be benevolent. Any student of history who cannot recognise in the eighteen years of Louis Napoleon's reign an era of genuine progress, enlightenment, culture, and social brilliancy, unmatched by any other two decades in the history of France, before or since, has other standards for these qualities to which sensible men, outside contemporary Russia, cannot possibly subscribe. The initiative and driving power for all the manifold cultural activities during those years came from one man—the Emperor Napoleon III. He has been described by a thousand pens as a Man of Mystery, a Sphinx, a dreamer, as well as an unprincipled adventurer. But remembering his passion for France, his industry, his close attention to every detail of the public service, his interest in science, commerce and manufacture, his improvements of Paris, the noble avenues, parks and public monuments directly inspired by him, the splendour of his Court, his amiable manners, and the mildness of his rule, one can only marvel at the ingratitude and caprice of the multitude. Surely a philosopher might exclaim: This little man toiling night and day in a single stuffy apartment in the Tuileries at his self-appointed task of making France richer, more respected and happier than he found it; to extend his country's interests and increase its influence—this man surely is no mystery. Here is no sphinx: rather he offers that spectacle which proverbially excites universal compassion—that of a good man struggling with adversity. The adversity suffered by Napoleon III consisted in the perpetual misunderstanding of his character, the suspicion of his motives, the refusal of foreign nations and nine-tenths of his own subjects to trust him, to admire him, to applaud him, or to see anything particularly meritorious in his conduct or in any action of his life. It was an ungrateful job while it lasted and posterity has not noticeably lightened the odium.

"He was called a dreamer," wrote one American who knew him intimately for twenty years, "and so he was in the sense in which the word can be applied to a political idealist—to a man incessantly thinking

—whose mind is engrossed and preoccupied by social and economic problems. But he was very far from being a dreamer who cherished illusions, or wasted his time in idle speculations. He kept very close to his facts in all his thinking—never reasoning far ahead of them after the manner of visionaries and so-called philosophers.

"The Emperor's mind was pre-eminently a practical one. From early youth he was only fond of those studies that had utilitarian ends in view; questions relating to government, to the army, to political economy, to sociology—whatever might contribute to the well-being of the people. There was never a detail so small concerning any of these subjects which, if new to him, failed to interest him. He was also unusually anxious to know all that was to be learned about ingeniously constructed machinery and useful inventions of every kind. He had a great admiration for these things. This, he acknowledged to me, was one of his principal reasons for having a very high opinion of Americans. On my showing him, one day, a mechanical device which a New York gentleman had requested me to submit to him, he said, after examining it carefully, and expressing his appreciation of the skill of the inventor, 'You Americans are sensible enough not to permit yourselves to be bound hand and foot by the usages and customs of centuries. Your aim is to accomplish what you do with the least expenditure of force—to econo-

mise labour and time; and it is by such economies
that industrial and social progress is made possible.' " *

It is a moot point as to whom amongst a great man's
immediate entourage one should go for a just estimate
of his character. His valet has long since been ruled
out. The testimony of his wife and children is suspect.
His secretary is apt to see only the taskmaster, while
his physician must be influenced by pathological fac-
tors and his own professional responsibility for the
functioning of the bodily machine. Dr. Fell, for all we
know, may have been both perspicuous and propitia-
tory, but he was not beloved. He did not invite confidence: to do that supremely one must be a dentist, and,
of course, an American dentist. The Court dentist of
Napoleon III then, astute, receptive of impressions,
manifestly had the root of the matter in him; was not
likely to be deceived by an imposing façade or mistake the quality of what is behind the tricks and graces
of human utterance.

His name was Thomas W. Evans, a plump and
competent Pennsylvanian in his early forties, whose
fluent side-whiskers were in the most approved style
of the period.

* *Memoirs of Dr. T. W. Evans.*

"It sometimes happens," reported the American Consul-General in Paris to Secretary Seward, "when the crowned heads of Europe wish to communicate with one another without any responsibility they send for Dr. Evans to fix their teeth."

In such cases the Doctor's services, though dental, were never accidental. He was known in the most exalted circles to be well-informed, discreet and trustworthy. When the war broke out, Dr. Evans had many Southern patients and for months it needed all his tact to arrest any decay of their confidence. But his natural Northern partisanship could not be wholly concealed, and when it became known that both the Emperor and the Empress were regular recipients of views and arguments favourable to the North, Secessionist suspicion and disfavour followed. Nevertheless, he persevered, for, as he says, "he knew the Emperor's mind was in danger of being poisoned by falsehoods emanating from a hundred sources in Paris which a true word spoken in season could dispel." Napoleon, on his side, found Evans very useful in supplying him with current intelligence.

"The Emperor," testified the Doctor, "while holding fast to what his judgment had approved, was slow to form opinions. He wished to examine every side of the question under consideration; and he commonly took the time to do so. He was very fond of asking questions about subjects in which he took interest, of any one who he supposed might be able to throw light upon them—even if it were only a sidelight. This habit was doubtless, in part, a matter of temperament, but it was a habit that was strengthened by having a practical end in view—he wished to form his own opinions; and, consequently, to see for himself what was to be seen, and in doing this he liked particularly to look into the dark corners of things. Indeed, in all matters of public concern he sought for information, when he could, at first hand, with a view of obtaining such a direct and personal knowledge of things as would enable him, should there be occasion, to check off, as it were, the more formal information that came to him through official sources, and thus more clearly understand its real value and significance. Credited by the world with being an absolute and responsible sovereign, he had no wish to be the slave of his own bureaucracy."

Elsewhere in his *Memoirs* Evans says:

"His cautiousness, his slowness, his hesitancy to come to a decision were in striking contrast with the boldness and swiftness with which he acted when he had finally decided upon the course to be taken, and felt that the opportune moment had come. Having resolved to accomplish a purpose, to reach

an object, he was prompt to move. Were the undertaking difficult or dangerous to execute, his activity
was prodigious, his self-control extraordinary, and
the reserve of energy upon which he drew apparently inexhaustible."

Such was Napoleon III, the man who now controlled the destinies of France, an ambitious but
thoughtful, prudent, patient man, ready to be convinced by argument, but unlikely to act unless certain
that all the circumstances rendered success certain.
No enthusiast, no dreamer, no mystic, but a practical man; what we call today a realist. Still as capable
of taking big risks as on the day he walked out of
prison at Ham in a workman's smock, a pipe in his
mouth and a plank on his shoulder. But the risk in
every case must be balanced by contingencies whose
occurrence would offset failure or make present delay jeopardise future success.

Thus it was in the case of the American Confederacy. It is the custom to call his knowledge of America superficial. One epigrammatic historian observes
that "having spent six weeks in a Broadway hotel he
cherished the illusion that he knew America." Louis
Napoleon's knowledge of America was so far from
superficial that it astonished many enlightened and
widely-travelled Americans. It elicited the grudging

admission of Laboulaye that the Emperor daily referred to De Tocqueville's pages in the light of M.
Mercier's despatches. He read the narratives of English and French travellers in America the moment
they were published; he frequently quoted Stuart's
Travels in North America, and the volumes of Basil
Hall and Mrs. Trollope. Copies of the Boston *Tran-
script* and the New York *Herald* and the New Orleans
Delta, as well as the *Courrier des Etats-Unis* were
often observed on his desk, with passages marked by
his own hand: and, evidence still more valid, he
showed a familiarity with the published Congressional
Debates which occasionally embarrassed a visiting
American legislator.

Slidell was not unaware of this. In Montgomery he
had spoken with C. J. Faulkner, the Virginian who
had been American Minister in Paris at the outbreak
of the war, who assured him of Napoleon's intimate
knowledge of political conditions and tendencies in
America. Another Virginian, M. F. Maury, an eminent hydrographer, who had had a three hours' interview with the Emperor in 1860, offered further
evidence:

> "After having exhausted all the little information
> I could afford him, draining me *à sec,* and leaving
> me, after all, under the impression that he knew

more of all the subjects on which he had examined me than I did myself, he turned with peculiar and undisguised eagerness to the Mexican question. I had then just returned from Cuba and fancied I had thoroughly informed myself as to the condition of things there and in the Gulf. I was soon undeceived. He knew the very number of guns in the Morro, the sums the United States had spent on the fortifications in Florida, the export and imports of Galveston and Matamoras, in short everything which well-informed local agents could have reported to an experienced statesman, eager for information. He examined me again on Texas and its population, the disposition of the French residents, the tendencies of the German colonists, the feeling on the Mexican frontier.... There were, of course, other points mentioned in a conversation carried on with his usual rapidity of thought and marvellous conciseness of expression, having a direct bearing on the question of French policy in the South."

When Napoleon first realized that the election of a Northern man, Lincoln, as President, made separation inevitable, he hoped that it might be accomplished without bloodshed. He never had much sympathy for the idea of a union of two elements so irreconcilable as the manufacturing democracy of the Northern and the rural aristocracy of the Southern States. He was opposed to slavery, but he thought that as practised

in the South it was on the whole humane and would
gradually, on economic grounds alone, be given up.
He did not believe the North would wage war on account of the slaves. His sympathies were naturally
with the South, not because he believed in what a later
generation calls "self-determination," but chiefly because he disliked and distrusted the "braggart democracy of the North." If he had acted in accordance with
his own feelings he would have acted precisely as
Louis XVI had acted with regard to the original Thirteen States, recognised the dozen Confederate States
and assisted them. He told Lord Cowley, the British
Ambassador, that "he never could forget the overbearing insolence of the United States Government in
its days of prosperity and hoped that they might receive a lesson." And any one today turning over the
pages of history must be struck by the many instances
in which American Presidents and Congresses have
affronted an astonished Europe and used the language
of arrogance and menace upon provocation which
would now be thought trivial, even upon no provocation at all.

Slidell, accompanied by young Eustis, arrived at the
beginning of February in Paris, whither his wife and
family had preceded him. On his arrival he was
greeted by several leading figures among the Southern

American residents of the capital, as well as by half a dozen eminent French sympathisers, amongst them M. de la Garonnière, a member of the Senate. At the railway station a number of zealous students, mostly from New Orleans, also had foregathered, with the idea of giving the representative of the new Confederacy a vociferous reception: but as their efforts threatened to involve a breach of the peace, after a single verse

> Bienvenu, notr' grand Slidell
> Au coeur loyale et l'âme fidèle:

they were induced by a couple of gendarmes to desist. Slidell, a dignified, bowing figure in "an enormous black felt hat," was driven rapidly across Paris to the Hotel du Rhin.

An apartment was later found for Slidell and his family at 25 Avenue d'Antin, since become, by one of those mutations of street nomenclature in which the Paris Municipal Council delights, the Avenue Victor Emmanuel. About the same time an office was rented in the adjacent rue Marignan.

Although the comparison always provoked Charles Sumner and the Abolitionists to wrath, yet there was much in Slidell's diplomatic entry into Paris to recall that of Benjamin Franklin in the previous century.

He, too, was without any recognised status, although secretly favoured by the reigning monarch; he, like Franklin, represented some millions of American "insurgents" engaged in casting off a hated political yoke: he, too, was denounced and regarded with suspicion by the official representative of the enemy. But there —or thereabouts—the comparison ends. Franklin's uphill battle for recognition lasted but for some months and he fought it with characteristic good humour: moreover, he came upon the scene himself a figure of international reputation, while John Slidell was a man unknown out of his own country.

Hardly had he been installed when a stream of callers of all ranks and nationalities began to flow towards him, making him aware of the presence not only of his own fellow-countrymen, but of a really large body of sympathisers with the Southern cause in Paris. Indeed, it may be said that the preponderance of public opinion, certainly among the upper classes, favoured the Confederacy on two and perhaps three counts. The first was a natural sympathy for a people believed to be more akin to the French themselves, of a culture and manners superior to the people of the North. *Nos frères de Louisiane* was a familiar phrase amongst pro-Southern Frenchmen. One recalls that Disraeli makes his Duke say in *Lothair,*

"You know, Colonel Campian is a gentleman; he is not a Yankee. People make the greatest mistakes about these things. He is a gentleman of the South; they have no property but land; and I am told his territory was immense. He has always lived in Paris and in the highest style."

The second point was that the war in America was another struggle for political independence. And thirdly, there was the fact that industrial France was dependent upon cotton from the South, whose seizure by the Federal blockaders was throwing thousands of French operatives out of work; and also upon Southern tobacco, both of which were exchanged for French silks. Added to these considerations was the belief that the success of the Confederacy would redound to France's prestige and political advantage.

Besides Persigny, de Morny, Fould and Rouher, Thouvenal, the Foreign Minister, while deprecating slavery and secession, also doubted the power of the North to restore the Union. (In England, the exiled Comte de Paris was of the same opinion.)

To the shrewdest European observers, like Anthony Trollope, Sir W. H. Russell and Cobden himself, the schism was permanent and would never be healed.

Altogether it was hardly surprising, as Mr. Pratt, co-author of *Europe and the American Civil War,* points out, that the Southern agents swarmed to Paris as the

> "best point from which to spread their propaganda. Two circumstances made it especially easy to circularise in France the usual arguments about slavery and separation. Parisian society was well acquainted with the charming type of Southern lady who with her husband and daughters frequently made her home in Paris. Many Frenchmen, disillusioned Republicans and now strong Imperialists, had a temperamental aversion to American democracy. The United States aroused in these people a feeling exactly opposite to that held by the *noblesse* who had responded so warmly to the Declaration of Independence. The lawless democracy which America incarnated was to them anathema. The Empire *autoritaire* had, they believed, no lesson to learn from America, but rather a lesson in governmental order and stability to teach to demogogic Union politicians and a lesson in Latin American statecraft to teach the American filibusters. Indeed, the Emperor's Mexican policy would of itself have made these Imperialists pro-Southern."

At the same time, no large body of articulate public opinion existed in France, as it did in England. In the *Corps Legislatif* the debates on American affairs provoked no particular heat. Billault, the Government spokesman, saw to it that the Imperial régime and policy were not compromised. In the Paris press, however, there was freer play, and the official and semi-official organs did not stint their language. Slidell had not been a week in Paris before he had met M. de La Gueronnière, the proprietor, and Aucaigne, the editor, of *La Patrie;* Cassagnac of *Le Pays;* and a leading contributor to *Le Constitutionnel,* of which journal Persigny was proprietor, and other journalists. As for *Le Moniteur,* although it seemed neutral and correct, yet the fact is that its news columns published so many "canards" of Confederate victories and Northern reverses and omitted so many events of vital importance, such as Lincoln's Emancipation Proclamation, as to induce a suspicion of its secret sympathies; it never failed to express the official opinion that American re-union was impossible.

Although the *Moniteur* was subtly pro-Southern, *Le Pays* was openly from the first a champion of the Confederacy and States' Rights. As to emancipation of the blacks, that might come in due time, slowly, peacefully and by mutual consent. If this "Puritan crusade against the Catholics of the South" succeeded, it would only produce another Ireland, another Venetia, another Poland. Meanwhile the Government of the United States "is one of the most barbarous, most ferocious and most inept which has ever been seen."

La Patrie was even more violently partisan for the South; *Le Constitutionnel* also came out for the Confederacy, whose course was one of "individual liberty, freedom of nationality and freedom of trade"; *L'Union,* the Clerical organ, was also on the side of the Secessionists. Taking the Northern side in the quarrel were *Le Siècle, Le Temps, Le Journal des Débats, La Presse* and *l'Opinion Nationale.* But the real strength of the Union cause, and especially as regards slavery, was rather to be found in the books, pamphlets and magazine articles by de Tocqueville, Thiers, Henri Martin, Ampère, Cochin, Laboulaye and Louis Blanc and in the influence wielded by Prince Napoleon ("Plon-Plon") and the Orleanist princes. The former in particular, who directly controlled *Le Siècle* and *La Presse* and who had visited America in 1861, made his house in Paris a centre and rallying-place for Northern partisans and made no secret of his entire disagreement with the opinions and policy of his Imperial cousin, and of Persigny. As regards the Liberal press, it may be added that the censorship was frequently exercised and many articles embarrassing to the policy of the Tuileries were rigorously suppressed.

French statesmen and the Paris press, although attaching importance to the sensational seizure of

LE SAUVAGE. _De grâce, messieurs ......, mettez y des formes !..... des formes !!.....
on ne s'égorge pas ainsi chez nous !....._

North and South
(From Charivari 1862)

Slidell and his fellow Commissioner, took it with calmness. If the incident led to war between England and the United States it was certain that France, as well as the new Confederacy, stood to gain.

At the moment of Slidell's arrival he found to his surprise the burning topic of the *Trent* already extinguished and submerged in the new Yankee outrage, the blocking of the port of Charleston. This was represented as the permanent ruin of the harbour by the sinking of stone-freighted ships at its mouth. The Governments of both France and England had issued a protest against this proceeding and it was even announced that France had instructed her Minister at Washington, Mercier, that she would in consequence no longer recognise the blockade of the Southern ports, that the stopping up of the harbour of Charleston was quite uncalled-for had the blockade been really effective.

It was not easy for Slidell to master current Continental political problems and their bearing on the fortunes of the Confederacy. As long as the Emperor's hands were tied he could hardly be expected to enter upon fresh commitments. There was Italy, for example, a vexatious business, rendered worse by the attitude of the Empress, whose reproaches were common gossip in diplomatic circles. In the previous year, Victor Emmanuel had been proclaimed King of a united Italy, but Rome and Venice still remained to be liberated; the Pope held fast to the former and Austria to Venice. In June, 1861, Cavour had died, murmuring "A free Church in a free State" with his last breath, leaving the task of liberation to Garibaldi. But Napoleon regarded himself as the champion of the Papal States and continued to garrison Rome with French troops. He realised that in doing so and in supporting the annexation of Venice, he was running counter to the pro-Italian sympathies of Europe, yet he had his reasons. Austria he distrusted and felt that "were Italy to make an aggressive move on Venice and be worsted, France might be obliged to take part in the war to prevent a subjugation of Italy." Such a war would be highly unpopular in France. Why should he again tempt fortune when no real necessity existed?

All through his first summer in Paris, Slidell heard rumours of connubial and ministerial differences of opinion with regard to the Roman question. At a dinner party at M. Fould's, Paiva, the Portuguese Minister, described a scene at the Tuileries, when the Empress confronted him like a tigress, asking what his master could mean by even thinking of marrying the daughter of "that man, Victor Emmanuel"?

Paiva was overcome by the suddenness of the attack and had to be reassured by the Emperor. The upshot of this was a domestic quarrel, followed by a reconciliation. As Cowley reported: "She promises no more scenes and he that the Pope shall not be abandoned."

But the divisions in the Cabinet were not so easily disposed of. Slidell had attached particular importance to the Council which was to meet at St. Cloud on October 15. He believed that at last official recognition was imminent. Even Thouvenel, so long lukewarm or averse, admitted that the time had come. The ministers met. What happened was thus reported by Slidell to Benjamin (20th October, 1862):

> "I had hoped before this to have it in my power to communicate something definite as to the Emperor's intentions respecting our affairs but new complications in the Italian question have entirely absorbed the attention of the Government. M. Thouvenel has resigned and has been succeeded by M. Drouyn de Lhuys. For two or three days, a general disruption of the cabinet was imminent. Messrs. de Persigny and Fould tendered their resignations, which if accepted would have been followed by two or three others. They were however induced to withdraw them by the earnest appeal of the Emperor and at present it seems probable that no further change will take place in the ministry."

Slidell goes on to say that he had now reason to be less hopeful of early joint recognition by France and England.

"Some days past I learned from an English friend that Lord Cowley (the British Ambassador) declared most emphatically that his Government had no official knowledge of the Emperor's views on the subject of recognition—that he had spoken, it was true, very freely to various persons of his warm sympathies for the South but that such conversations had no public significance and until he gave them an official form her Majesty's Ministers would be presumed to be ignorant of them. I have entire reliance on the truthfulness of the gentleman who gave me this information coming directly to him from Lord Cowley. On enquiring at the *Affaires Etrangères* I was informed by the friend to whom I have alluded in previous dispatches, that M. Thouvenel expressed great surprise at Lord Cowley's assertion, saying that it had to him the appearance of a *'mauvaise plaisanterie'*: that there had been between the two governments *'des pourparlers tres réels'* on the subject of American affairs; that England was not as well disposed to act as the Government of the Emperor; that it was from London that a communication was expected and that the object of France was to bring about an armistice as a necessary preliminary to peace. Lord Lyons was decidedly opposed to any action until the result of the Northern elections should have been ascertained, and his views would probably prevail in the Cabinet, shortly to be held, when the tenor of the instructions to be given him would be decided. The discrepancy between the statements of Lord Cowley and M. Thouvenel is such, that giving, as I do, full credence to the latter, I can only suppose that Lord Cowley is not kept informed by his Government or that he deliberately misrepresents the position of affairs; on this alternative I do not venture to express opinion."

Slidell had long been disappointed with Thouvenel and he welcomed the Change in Foreign Ministers.

"M. Drouyn de Lhuys had always been understood to be very favourably disposed towards our cause.
"After the first interchange of courtesies I said I had been pleased to hear from various quarters that I should not have to combat with him the adverse sentiments that had been attributed to his predecessor with what degree of truth I did not permit myself to appreciate."

THE titular chief of the Northern camp in Paris was the Federal Minister William L. Dayton, who had arrived the previous May in succession to the Southerner Faulkner. Dayton was a New Jersey lawyer, formerly Republican candidate for the Vice-Presidency. Although a man of character and ability, he was prosaic, timid and lacking in magnetism. Almost his first step had been to report to Seward that

> "our Legations and Consulates had been filled largely, not to say exclusively, during the administration of President Buchanan, with men of more or less doubtful loyalty, and London and Paris were swarming with Confederate emissaries. The officials and unofficials were all equally active in propagating the impression that the insurgent States had been wronged and oppressed by the Washington Government; that the Confederates were fighting only for their common rights, and not for slavery; that disunion was inevitable and imminent, and that neither the Washington Government nor the people of the loyal States in the impending quarrel had any just claim to the sympathies or respect of any foreign Power."

To counter this propaganda he asked that some competent person be sent to Paris, and so a few months later there had descended upon the boulevards —or rather re-descended—for he had sojourned in Paris and met a number of influential people just before the war—an able and energetic New York journalist. His name was John Bigelow and he had long been associated with William Cullen Bryant in the control of the *Evening Post,* from which he had just retired in the prime of life with a considerable fortune. When Bigelow patriotically offered his services to the Government he was promptly appointed Consul-General at Paris, a title which cloaked his activities as literary propagandist-in-chief of the United States in Europe. These activities were so incessant and so comprehensive as almost to render those of the Minister superfluous. Dayton could not help feeling this, but it was difficult for him, owing to Bigelow's intimate relations with Seward and Sumner, to resent it.

Dayton, with his wife and son, had an apartment in the Rue Circulaire at the Etoile and there he had established the Legation. His Secretary of Legation was a young man named Pennington, who had been personally known to Slidell at Washington during his secretaryship. Bigelow's opinion of Pennington he subsequently conveyed to the Secretary of State.

> "His ignorance is profound; he has neither the desire nor the capacity to learn anything; his habits are not very good; he is careless and untidy in his person and boorish in his manners; he writes an illegible hand and is incapable of inditing the simplest sort of note in a satisfactory way."

There are far too many counts in this indictment. Pennington was quite a personable fellow and not without certain talents, as will be seen later.

Pennington naturally resented the irruption of Bigelow as superseding in many directions his own chief; and if at times the relations between the tall, angular, energetic Consul-General, who spoke and wrote French with facility and corresponded freely with Cabinet officers and dignitaries, and the portly, elderly, easy-going Minister whose literary and linguistic gifts were so limited, became slightly strained, the Secretary did nothing to ease matters. As for Pennington and Bigelow they hardly spoke to one another: and the former did his best to induce his chief to "put the great Mr. John Bigelow in his proper place." *

To counteract Bigelow's efforts, Secretary Benjamin wrote to Slidell:

> "I have arrived at the conclusion that a sufficient sum of secret service money has not hitherto been placed at the disposal of our diplomatic agents abroad. With enemies so active, so unscrupulous; and with a system of deception so thoroughly organized as that now established by them abroad, it becomes absolutely essential that no means be spared for the dissemination of truth, and for a fair exposition of our condition and policy before foreign nations. It is not wise to neglect public opinion, nor prudent to leave to the voluntary interposition of

* Letter from Pennington, Nov. 17, 1863, to Congressman Davis.

friends, often indiscreet, the duty of vindicating our country and its cause before the tribunal of civilised man. The President sharing these views has authorised me to place at your disposal twenty-five thousand dollars which you will find to your credit with Messrs. Fraser, Trenholm & Co. of Liverpool,* and which you will use for the service of your country in such way as you may deem most judicious, with special view however to the necessity of the enlightenment of public opinion in Europe through the Press."

Socially, it was soon apparent enough that the United States Legation was at a disadvantage as compared with the Confederate mission in the Avenue d'Antin, and Parisian society quickly recognised that fact. Slidell's presence, bearing and speech gave him an advantage over his official adversary, and in George Eustis and subsequently Henri Vignaud, he had attractive and competent lieutenants. But his chief asset was his wife, the former Mademoiselle Mathilde Deslonde, and their two pretty daughters Matilda and Rosina.† There was also a son, Alfred, still a schoolboy and afterwards a cadet at St. Cyr.‡

* Bankers throughout to the Confederacy.
† These later became Madame d'Erlanger and the Comtesse de St. Roman. The latter's daughter is today the wife of General Marchand of Fashoda fame.
‡ He died in 1920.

Mrs. Slidell, intelligent, sympathetic, with charming manners and a gift for music and water-colour painting, made friends easily. According to her daughter she was "profoundly religious, austere towards herself, indulgent to others." She had been highly esteemed as a hostess in Washington and she soon occupied her due place in Paris. The girls were fond of music, the opera and dancing, as was the secretary Eustis's young and charming wife, the rich banker's daughter.

But there were lions in the social path of the Slidells. Many hostesses were Légitimistes and traditionally on the side of the Union, and the two Orléanist princes had actually gone to America to serve on McClellan's staff.

Others were timid or were dissuaded by their husbands from openly showing their sympathies for the South. The case of one lady was widely discussed. She gave a grand evening party at which both the Daytons and Slidells had been invited. The moment the American Minister had discovered the presence of the "rebel" Commissioner he had ordered his carriage. But Slidell, by an adroit movement, had anticipated him. On this occasion the girls were left behind on the tearful protestation of their hostess that if they went a large number of her guests would follow and also

From the painting by George Healy

Mrs. John Slidell
(Née Mathilde Deslonde)

that two of her star performers would refuse to sing!

A number of Southern ladies, the Calhouns, Corbins, Souters, Buchanans and Hamptons had already formed a Confederate Woman's Aid Society, for the collection of drugs, clothing and comforts for the Southern wounded and prisoners.

There was also a group which organised bazaars, and gave musicales and popular concerts in the same cause; of these a leading spirit was a vivacious soubrette from New Orleans, lately a pupil at the Conservatoire, named Sophie Bricard. She had already exhibited herself as a stormy petrel and her singing of *La Bannière Bleue, Salut O mon pays! Aide-Nous, O France aimée!* moved audiences to a delirium of excitement. After several public appearances as an amateur, Mademoiselle Bricard at length obtained an engagement at the Bouffes-Parisiens, the little theatre which Jacques Offenbach had transformed and rendered amazingly successful with a long series of clever and tuneful operettas.

The character of some of the Southern gatherings in Paris may be judged from the following cover of the programme of one of them:

SALLE DOURLANS
Avenue de Wagram
Wednesday, June 3rd, 1863.
Reunion and Concert under the auspices
of the Societies of the Sons of
the South and The Daughters of the South
in Honor of
the Birthday of his Excellency
The Honorable JEFFERSON DAVIS
President of the Confederate States
of America

Chairman: Hon. John Slidell,
Commissioner to France of the
Confederate States.
Speakers: Colonel A. Dudley Mann; Judge Eustis.
Vocalists: Miss Corbin, Miss Buchanan, Mr. Post.
At the Piano: Miss M. Slidell.

The speeches delivered on these occasions were of
the florid order then demanded by American audiences, both North and South, at home or abroad, and
which had in Dudley Mann a facile exponent.

Sometimes there were original songs and recitations,
replete with patriotism and pathos, but with never a
trace of humour, except indeed of the unconscious
variety. The Southerners were too much in earnest for
that. The light-hearted Yankee soldiers might "hang

Jeff Davis to a sour-apple tree," but south of Mason and Dixon's line Abraham Lincoln appeared a sinister, never a comic figure, and the triumphant Confederate march into Pennsylvania was set to no such rollicking measure as was the Federal invasion of Georgia. As a sample of the prevailing sentiment in poetry the following specimen, "words and music by a young Southern gentleman living in Paris," may be given:

MY LAD IN GRAY

He came to me one morning,
The Lad I loved in Gray,
A sword was girdled round his waist,
I could not say him nay,
He clasped me close against his breast,
And then—he rode away.

They bore him back one evening,
The Lad I loved in Gray,
His temples bound to hide the wound,
His cheek the hue of clay,
He gave a sigh: "Before I die
I have this word to say,

"I fought for you and Dixie
I donned my country's gray,
I gave my life, I lost my wife,
But Dixie lives for aye.
Serve her for me, but till she's free
Wed ne'er a Lad in Gray!"

During three years Slidell had various colleagues, associates and helpers, including the emissaries sent over from time to time by the Richmond Government. Of the three original Confederate Commissioners to Europe only one, Dudley Mann, remained, and he only in a quasi-official capacity, living in England with occasional trips to the continent. There were half a dozen propagandists, led by Commander M. F. Maury, James Spence, Henry Hotze, Edwin de Leon and Aucaigne, besides amateur enthusiasts like John Arthur Roebuck, M.P., and James Lindsay, M.P., who were often in Paris.

In a different category from these were the two agents of the Confederate Navy and War Departments, Captain J. D. Bulloch and Major Caleb Huse.

When the War broke out Bulloch, a Georgian and ex-naval officer, was in command of a United States mail steamer plying between New York and New Orleans. He at once volunteered for service in the Confederate Navy, returned his steamer to its owners in New York and made his way to Montgomery, Alabama, where he presented himself to Mallory, Secretary of the Navy.

"I am glad to see you, Captain Bulloch," said this personage. "I want you to go to Europe. When can you start?"

"I have no impedimenta," was the prompt reply, "and can start as soon as you explain what I am to do."

Mallory did not expect a formal recognition of the Confederacy as an independent Power until its probable success had been demonstrated by some substantial victories in the field, but he thought that England and France would grant the commissioned cruisers of the South the shelter and privileges conceded to all belligerents by the comity of nations. He warned Bulloch to be prudent and heedful in the operations he would be charged to undertake, so as not to involve the diplomatic agents of the Confederacy in embarrassing complaints for alleged violation of neutrality, and advised him to study carefully the terms of the neutral proclamations which would certainly be issued. The banking firm, Fraser, Trenholm & Co., of Liverpool, would advance him money for the purchase of suitable cruisers and naval supplies.

At sea the Confederacy was at a great disadvantage as compared with the Northern States. The latter had four ample, well-equipped dockyards, many home ports and facilities abroad. Throughout the conflict now to ensue the Confederate cruiser was deprived of any home port for outfit or retreat. "Her flag was tolerated only, not recognised. Once upon the seas she could never hope to re-supply the continual waste of her powers of offence or defence, and could obtain but a grudging allowance of the merest necessaries. Her military chest was the paymaster's safe and her financial resources were the moderate supply of sovereigns with which she began her cruise. In case of difficulty there was no resident Minister to whom the captain could refer for counsel or support, no consular representative who could set his case before the authorities in the neutral ports." *

While in England and France the Confederate cruisers received fair and courteous treatment, in the distant colonies or the ports of other countries everything depended on the local authorities and the personal pressure the United States consul could bring to bear. Nevertheless, the Confederacy could always command the services of a numerous, skilled and intrepid body of men whose daring exploits afloat form the theme of several thrilling volumes. In the face of truly appalling difficulties, Bulloch succeeded in getting the *Florida* and the *Alabama* built in England, as well as four ironclads which he failed to get afloat, and to purchase many other craft and a vast quantity of naval stores and material, despite the protests and unremitting activities of the United States Minister to England, Charles Francis Adams.

* Bulloch.

But Bulloch's preliminary activities in England do not concern these pages. At first the Confederate Government had concentrated their hopes and their efforts upon England and continued to do so until the obstacles placed in their way and the changed policy of the Government brought about disillusion and disappointment.

Major Caleb Huse was a West Point graduate, who after serving a number of years in the Artillery had retired from active service and accepted the post of commandant of the Alabama State Military Academy. The fact that this trained officer was actually living at the state capital, Montgomery, when the Confederate Provisional Government was formed there, had an immediate effect upon Huse's fortunes. Secretary Benjamin saw that he was just the man they wanted. He was therefore immediately despatched to Europe to purchase arms and ordnance supplies as the official agent of the War Department and Ordnance Bureau, and there he remained throughout the War.

Captain Bulloch testifies to Huse's ability and energy. "I have always felt," he says, "that the safety of Richmond at the time of General McClellan's advance from Yorktown up the Peninsula in the Spring of 1862 was largely due to Prioleau [the banker] * and Huse, because the former furnished the credits and the latter bought and forwarded the rifles and field artillery without which the great battles of Seven Pines and the Chickahominy could not have been successfully fought." ... Huse grew expert in pressing the credit of the Government and in making large contracts and getting delivery of arms and other ordnance stores, when no ready money was obtainable. Although England was at first the scene of Huse's operations, he came frequently to France, Belgium, Germany and elsewhere on the Continent wherever arms and munitions were to be had. Eventually, as we shall see, he took a house at Auteuil, near Paris.

Besides these men, the office in the Rue Marignan was the rendezvous of a miscellaneous assortment of secret agents, commission merchants, journalists and, at times, an embarrassing number of naval and military men either actively employed or desiring employment in the Confederate service. Of such were Commodore Barrow, Captain W. F. Maury and Captain Moffitt, of whom more hereafter.

Then there were the secret service agents. Had Slidell not in 1866 destroyed a list containing the names of nearly one hundred of these persons who

* Of the firm of Fraser, Trenholm & Co.

were paid from time to time for supplying information or rendering services to the Confederate Government, it would reveal as fine a collection of venal
rogues as were ever employed by Talleyrand and
Fouché. Several of them were actually in the French
Government service: one, a respected official at the
Quai d'Orsay, received a regular subsidy to report on
the letters and visits of the American Minister in Paris
and on diplomatic correspondence generally relating
to American affairs. But by far the greater number
were literary men and journalists, not always in Paris,
or even in France.

Then there were the dangerous gentlemen who
offered their services to the Confederacy as spies,
assassins and incendiaries. A translation by George
Eustis of a letter addressed to Slidell by a Frenchman
long resident in America gives one an idea of the
violence some of these fanatics were ready to perpe-
trate.

"Marseilles, September 28th 1863
"HON. JOHN SLIDELL,
"SIR,
    "I venture to address you as a French citizen who
has resided in the city of Charleston for over eleven
years and is heart and soul for the cause of the Confederacy. In the months which I passed in the towns
and cities of the North, especially Boston, I am con-

vinced that these people will stop at no measure, however infamous or blood-thirsty to effect the ruin of your country. What I fear is that your Government will be too lenient, too humane. You cannot afford to neglect any means to strike terror into their hearts. It will not do to wait until you have ships to bombard Boston or New York. The same result could be attained by a band of fearless men, who assembling in Canada could easily cross the border, join the gangs of forced conscripts who now parade the streets at night and armed only with petrol bombs ignite the principal buildings.... I would not hesitate to offer myself and several of my friends in that splendid enterprise which is certain to be crowned with success.... Not only the material, but the moral effect is to be considered.... The City Hall and Cooper's Union hall would offer a good beginning....

"If you embrace this proposal I will come to Paris with two of my companions and exhibit you a plan in detail." *

In 1861 President Lincoln had sent to Russia as Minister Plenipotentiary a distinguished anti-slavery Kentuckian, Cassius Marcellus Clay. On the heels of this it was announced that the Confederate Government had appointed Captain M. F. Maury, a Naval officer and scientist of international repute, as its Com-

* Eustis Papers.

missioner in St. Petersburg. It was believed that Napoleon's overtures to the Tsar in respect to mediation might be favourably received and Slidell himself agreed with this, while observing that it was a pity Maury had not been appointed earlier.

Maury came to London and Paris, looked about him and declined diplomacy on those terms.

In place of Maury, another envoy from Richmond presented himself in the Avenue d'Antin en route to St. Petersburg. This was Lucius Quintus Curtius Lamar, a Mississippi lawyer. One might suspect that another Roman prenomen was called for merely to counter-balance the effect of Cassius Marcellus Clay; but Lamar was really an able man. He bore letters from President Davis assuring the Tsar of the good will of the Confederacy and the desire for commercial relations. Missions of Southern gentlemen to Russia were disappointing affairs, as John Randolph of Virginia had found out to his cost nearly forty years before, and this was to be no exception. Lamar struck Paris as an imposing, even picturesque personality, and in his broad-brimmed hat, tightly-buttoned frock coat, and hirsute luxuriance he cut a striking figure on the boulevards. Slidell gave a dinner party in his honour and introduced him to several persons intimate with Russian affairs, and in particular a leading mem-

ber of the Russian colony in Paris. Lamar explained
that he attached great importance to coming to a
friendly arrangement with Russia and so offsetting
the overtures Seward had been making to the Tsar's
government which were founded on a complete
misapprehension of Northern designs on Russian
America.

All that was very well, said his Russian acquaintance, but what about slavery? Slavery, replied Lamar,
was not an issue: at least it was purely domestic: he
should say nothing about that. On the contrary, declared his informant, with the Tsar it was the only
issue, just as it was in England and France. Lamar,
who cared nothing about slavery, wrote at once to
Davis and was told to come home; the Senate had
refused to confirm his appointment. Lamar was not
unprepared for his recall, for, as he wrote Benjamin,

> "after frequent consultation with Messrs. Mason and
> Slidell ... I had almost reached the determination
> of recommending to you that I should be released
> from my duties, or, at least, that they should be di-
> rected to another field. Although it could not be
> expected that the Government of Austria or Prussia
> would be prepared to take the initiative in recog-
> nition, there was yet good reason to believe that
> either or both these powers could be so far influenced

as to lend their moral weight to the efforts which are made in England and France. I acquiesce in the decision of the Senate the more readily since, in one respect at least, it anticipates by a few days the conclusion I was about to communicate to you."

He was told that in consequence of their reports about the attitude of Europe, the Confederate Government doubted the advantage of having any Commissioners abroad at all. Concerning this Lamar wrote Benjamin:

"I trust, however, you will not consider me as going out of my way when I urge that the principle which has governed this decision not be extended to the withdrawal of diplomatic representatives at London and Paris, as the proceedings in the House of Representatives and the tone of the press lead me to apprehend. The presence of these gentlemen at their respective posts is imperiously demanded by exigencies of the public service, even though the main object of their mission may not, for some time to come, be carried out against the prejudiced obstinacy of the English Foreign Office or the languor which has recently characterized the Imperial policy in American affairs."

CHAPTER III

SLIDELL ENCOUNTERS THE EMPEROR

ABOUT a fortnight after Slidell's arrival he met the Emperor under the most singular and dramatic circumstances. He had been induced to lend his patronage to Mademoiselle Sophie Bricard by taking a box for her début at the Bouffes-Parisien theatre. But the day before the première of *Florian* there arrived a message from the Court Chamberlain intimating that his Majesty the Emperor would attend. There were only two *avant-scène* loges at the Bouffes-Parisien and the second was permanently reserved for Offenbach's patron, the Duc de Morny, whose permission would first have to be obtained before it could be given to Mr. Slidell. Almost at the same time a gentleman appeared from the American Legation, desiring to secure a stage-box for the Minister and Mrs. Dayton. Although the Duc de Morny was, it appeared, ready to yield his box to Mrs. Slidell and party, yet a higher

authority intervened—the Emperor himself—and a
voucher for the box was sent to Mr. Dayton. After
this, there was nothing left for the Confederate Commissioner but to recognise the protocol and accept
three seats in the stalls. Even for these, three patrons
who had paid a high price for them were induced to
yield them—so great was the demand for the *première*.

The notable night arrived: and the house filled
rapidly with an unusually *chic* assemblage.

Although disappointed in obtaining a stage-box, the
Slidells and George Eustis occupied conspicuous seats
in the orchestra and were the centre of attraction to a
large body of their partisans in the house.

Slidell's florid, distinguished features and long iron-
grey hair marked him out as a personage of distinction. Twice before the curtain rose he was obliged to
rise and bow his acknowledgements of the applause of
his Southern admirers. This might have been tolerated; but some of the more zealous and noisy of these
persons seized upon the occasion of the Federal
Minister's entry to launch into a storm of hissing.
This was what the management had feared from the
first. Two gendarmes were immediately despatched to
bid the disturbers curb a demonstration which, if persisted in, would cause the Emperor, who was momen-
tarily expected, to leave the theatre instantly. The

warning had the desired effect. The display of bad manners ceased, and Mr. Dayton was called upon in turn to bow to Federal applause from his *loge*.

The new opera had a reception which, if not triumphant, was at least noisy, the Emperor joining in the plaudits accorded Mlle. Bricard, who, however, in the opinion of impartial critics, had only a mediocre talent, either as singer or actress. At the end of the second act, Slidell and his young secretary, Eustis, were invited to visit the green-room for the purpose of congratulating their fair compatriot. There, much to their surprise, they found that the Emperor had preceded them and that M. Offenbach, Mlle. Schneider and the company were being presented to his Majesty. When Mlle. Bricard's turn came, the Emperor smilingly took her hand. At that instant, the soubrette, catching sight of the Confederate Commissioner, turned towards him, and to the dismay of the company (there were altogether some dozen persons in the green-room), exclaimed,

"*Voilà, Sire, voilà le représentant de mon pays souffrant!* The South is fighting for freedom. On my knees, I supplicate your Majesty. Give us the friendship of France!"

At this startling outbreak, which was accompanied by appropriate dramatic action, the Emperor frowned

and retreated a step. But he was off his guard only for
a moment. Turning to Slidell, whom he had not previously met, he shook hands calmly. Then, without
another word, his Majesty left the green-room.

Behind the scenes Offenbach was furious. At the
close of the third act, it was remarked that the Emperor was no longer in his box. Quickly, it ran from
lip to lip that something extraordinary had happened
in the green-room, that his Majesty and the Confederate Minister had been brought together by *la petite
Bricard,* that Napoleon had avowed his sympathy with
the Secessionist cause, had raised the kneeling figure
of the beautiful Southern heroine and assured her that
France would shortly be at the side of her valiant
people! *

Whatever extravagant account was given currency
by the Southern party, the whole evening's proceedings gave deep umbrage to the Unionists in the American Colony in Paris. The following night a body of
young men (and a few women) repaired to the
Bouffes-Parisiens and loudly hissed Mlle. Bricard, a
free fight was narrowly averted and both factions were
nearly ejected from the theatre.

The American Minister, who had gone to the

* The whole of this version follows closely the MS. *The Death
of Minister Dayton,* R. P. 1869.

theatre from diplomatic and pacific motives, was extremely annoyed over the whole business and complained to the French Foreign Minister, who in turn notified the Prefect of Police that Mlle. Bricard must refrain from provocative sallies, such as carrying a Confederate flag in her bosom, emphasising certain ambiguous lines in her part and generally inciting a political manifestation.

At the close of the run of *Florian,* which was exceptionally brief, the little Bricard's professional career came to an end, and for three months she was not seen in Paris. During that time she became the wife of a young man named Eccles, about whom nothing today is known. Eventually he disappeared and was rumored to have joined Lee's army. It is probable that he left his wife or widow well-provided for, for Mrs. Eccles rented an apartment at the Louvre Hotel and gave frequent parties there to her admirers.

In the letter of a youthful American visitor to Paris, written early in 1864, occurs this passage:

"P. took me on Sunday night to one of Mrs. Eccles' receptions, formerly the notorious Sophie Bricard of New Orleans. Her apartment is fairly large and gaudily furnished. It is in a hotel close to the Théâtre Français. She is very petite, looks about twenty-five and has beautiful hair and eyes, but I

don't care much for her expression. Learning from
P. that I was from Missouri she was pleased to show
me flattering attention; but as she is a rabid Secessionist I guess it would have disgusted her to know
my real sentiments and that my two brothers are
just now fighting in Grant's army. There were several queer-looking customers about, said to be naval
men, but I suppose these regard Sophie's place a convenient rebel rendezvous. I must not forget to mention that there are large framed portraits of Jeff
Davis, Lee, Beauregard, Benjamin and the rest about
the place, and that the end of a big piano is draped
with a rebel flag."

On the 15th July, 1862, the Paris papers contained
an account of the defeat of the Federal armies before
Richmond and that same evening they were being
eagerly perused by the Emperor, then taking the
waters at Vichy. The news confirmed what he had
suspected for some months, that the young Northern
commander, General McClellan, in no wise possessed
the military genius of his Majesty's Imperial uncle, in
spite of the title "The Little Napoleon" which his admirers so handsomely bestowed upon him. The
Emperor distinctly remembered meeting young Captain McClellan, who had been presented to him a few
years before, together with a couple of other American
officers attending European manœuvres; he had since

followed his movements (or lack of movement) with particular attention. The recent military proceedings in America only confirmed the Emperor in his conviction that the ultimate success of the North was highly problematical. The Southern Confederacy was showing itself more than a match for its richer and more populous opponent. President Lincoln's call for 300,000 additional troops revealed the desperate nature of the situation.

In short, there now seemed little reason to delay giving an audience to the Commissioner of the Confederacy and discussing with him the subject of European intervention. The Comte de Persigny, being informed, wrote to Slidell strongly recommending to him an immediate indulgence in the healing waters of Vichy. The hint was taken, and on the very evening of Slidell's arrival, a note came from the Emperor's aide-de-camp, General Fleury, observing that it would be agreeable for his Majesty to receive Mr. Slidell whenever he should make his presence known. Slidell promptly replied and a rendezvous was fixed for the following day. At two o'clock the statesman from Louisiana arrived at the modest Imperial chalet and was shown into the Emperor's presence.

The latter's greeting of his visitor was very cordial. Although there was no allusion to any previous meeting it could hardly fail to have been in the minds of both. "So, Mr. Slidell," began the Emperor, pleasantly, referring to the news in the papers, "it is not going to be such a simple affair as your opponents imagined. They seem to have lost heavily."

This fact appeared, so Slidell reported to Benjamin, to give "much satisfaction" to the Emperor. He went on to assure his visitor that although it was to France's interest that the United States should be a powerful and united people, so as to act as a counterpoise to the maritime power of England, yet his own sympathies had always been with the South, "whose people are struggling for the principle of self-government," of which he declared he was a firm and consistent advocate. He had from the first seen the true character of the contest and "considered the re-establishment of the Union impossible and final separation a mere question of time." But, his Majesty went on, the difficulty was to find a way to give effect to his sympathies. He had always desired to preserve the most friendly relations with England and therefore in so grave a matter he had not been willing to act without her co-operation. He had several times intimated his wish for action in behalf of the South, but had met with no favourable response. "England has really a deeper interest in the question than we have, but she wishes me to draw the chestnuts from the fire for her benefit." Having thus stated his own position, the Emperor now asked Slidell to favour him with his own views upon the situation and what could be done to bring the war to a close.

Up to this point the conversation had been conducted in French, Napoleon at first assuming that as Slidell hailed from a former French colony he habitually spoke that tongue. But perhaps he had already begun to suspect a slight declension from the purest Parisian accent, and when Slidell begged that he might henceforth express himself in English ("which all the world knew his Majesty spoke well and fluently"), Napoleon smilingly assented.

"And now," said he, "tell me the number of men you have in the field?" Slidell put the number at 350,000. Although at first they had nearly half a million, the Confederacy had since adopted the policy of concentrating its military forces.

"Our difficulty is not to find men—of them we have and always will have more than enough; what we lack are arms, powder and clothing. With us every man is a soldier, and very many of the élite of our country are serving in the ranks." Slidell spoke of the devotion and enthusiasm of the Southern women, and of the men who, badly clothed and fed, most of them with inferior arms and all insufficiently and irregularly paid, submitted patiently to all privations.

What a contrast the armies of the North presented! —admirably equipped and armed, plentifully fed, having many luxuries in abundance, such as tea and coffee, of which the Confederate rank and file were entirely deprived.

"Not coffee!" ejaculated the Emperor. "Do you really mean to say the troops have no coffee ration?"

"Even so, Sire," responded Slidell, somewhat surprised that the absence of this fragrant beverage should excite special commiseration.

"Coffee," pronounced the Emperor, "is considered by us essential to the health of our soldiers." His visitor might have mentioned that the armies of his Majesty's uncle had managed a score of successful campaigns entirely without it, and that its introduction as an army ration synchronised with the year of its first defeats. But he was himself perhaps unaware of this.

"Probably one-half of the Northern troops," continued Slidell, "are foreigners, principally Germans and Irish, while our troops are almost exclusively born on our soil. This fact makes them more than a match for their enemies when they meet in equal numbers; but this advantage is more than compensated by the greater moral value of those whom we lose, for mourning is carried into every Southern home, while small interest is felt in the North for the mercenaries who are fighting their battles, so long as new levies can supply their places."

This contention seemed perfectly sound to Napoleon, who had recent American immigration statistics at his fingers' ends. After a few other observations, Slidell felt that he might now bring on the carpet the great scheme which his Government had charged him to propose. He had shown the Emperor the vastly superior resources of the North for obtaining war material and supplies, and the great disadvantage under which the Confederacy was placed by reason of its closed ports. If therefore an arrangement could be concluded by which French products could be introduced into the country, the Confederacy was prepared to permit their entry free of duty. What the South wanted was a Franco-Confederate treaty, which would solve all its difficulties. At the same time it was recognised that such a treaty would naturally involve France in grave obligations; a refusal to recognise the blockade would imply naval convoys for French merchant ships. To meet this expenditure, therefore, the South was prepared to hand over at once sixty million francs' worth of cotton as a subsidy to the French navy.

The Confederacy, it is true, would pay only twenty million francs for this cotton (100,000 bales), but it was worth thrice that sum in Europe. The vessels sent under convoy to receive the cotton subsidy would of course be loaded with cargoes of general French merchandise, worth five times as much in the South as in Europe, so that the profits to French merchants would mean another forty or fifty millions.

Thus the French finances, which Slidell had heard were just then giving profound anxiety to the Imperial Government, would find immediate and perhaps permanent relief; the idle cotton mills would revive, and the machinations of the North to starve the South into submission would be foiled.

Napoleon listened to all this with the deepest interest. The proposal did not seem disagreeable. "But," he enquired, "how am I to get this cotton?"

"That, of course, depends on your Majesty. You would soon have a fleet in the neighbourhood of our coast, strong enough to keep it clear of every Federal cruiser." After all, pursued Slidell, what was the American navy? Merely some second-class steamers constructed for war purposes and a large number of merchant vessels hastily purchased and fitted up for the blockade and transport service. Such warships as the *Gloire*, the *Garonne* or the *Normandie* could pass the fortifications of New York and Boston and hold those towns at their mercy, or could enter the Chesapeake, destroy all the vessels there and bombard Fortress Monroe to fragments.

The Emperor's eyes, small and commonly veiled, lit up with a strange animation. "True, true!" he murmured. Slidell followed up the topic. He expressed his regret at hearing that some of his Majesty's first-class ships were armed *en flute* and asked if their armament could not be completed at Martinique and Guadeloupe, or if not, could not guns be sent there for the purpose? Napoleon was "pleased with the suggestion." Is it any wonder that Slidell felt the thrill of approaching triumph?

"But recognition," mused the Emperor, as if communing with himself, "simple recognition would be of no value and mediation would be refused by the North."

To this Slidell responded:

"True, your Majesty, mediation would be refused by them, but it would be accepted by us and that fact would have enormous weight throughout the universe. All we ask for is recognition. There is a large majority in the Northern States in favour of peaceful separation, but they dare not express this sentiment save in New York, where there has lately been a great peace meeting. The Emperor's recognition would evoke similar demonstrations. Then, Sire," pursued Slidell, warming to the theme, "there is another consideration —the interests of humanity."

"Ah!" The Emperor pricked up his ears. Humanity—it had been dinned into his ears a good deal of late, especially by the Abolitionists and anti-slavery societies. Was it possible that M. Slidell was going to speak to him on the delicate subject of Southern slavery?

"Humanity"—repeated his interlocutor—"although we do not place ourselves on that ground—the interests of humanity call upon Europe and especially upon your Majesty, who exercises so potent an influence over the destinies of the world, to put an end to the present strife, which is not only devastating the South and exhausting the North, but has paralysed the industry and commerce of Europe."

"True," replied Napoleon drily, "but the policy of nations is controlled and rightly controlled, in my opinion, by their interests, and not by their sentiments."

The Louisianian could not well deny this proposition, but submitted that statesmen should look beyond the present hour. England had formerly played a great part, but now she seemed to have abdicated her former rôle, in favour of a tortuous, selfish and time-serving policy which made all nations her bitter enemies or merely fair weather friends.

"We of the South, Sire, were at first well-disposed towards England, but she having revived for selfish ulterior purposes the old exploded principles of a blockade, so as to secure a monopoly of cotton for her Indian possessions, and given a false interpretation of the Treaty of Paris, we can never hereafter regard her as our friend."

NAPOLEON: I have already told you what I think of the blockade and as to the culture of cotton in India supplanting yours I consider the idea entirely chimerical. If you do not give it to us we cannot find it elsewhere.

SLIDELL: Your Majesty has now an opportunity of securing a faithful ally, bound to you not only by the ties of gratitude, but by those, more reliable, of a common interest and congenial habits.

NAPOLEON: Yes: I believe you have many families of French descent in Louisiana who still preserve their national habits and language. But tell me, Mr. Slidell, do you anticipate *no* difficulty from your *slaves?*

Slaves—slavery. The visitor had been apprehensive of the conversation touching upon that topic. He hastily assured the Emperor that the slaves in the

South had never been quieter or more respectful, the best evidence of their being contented and happy. This (he reported to Benjamin) "was the only allusion made to slavery during the interview."

Returning to the subject of recognition the Emperor asked if Slidell expected that England would agree to co-operate with him. The Commissioner replied that his Majesty had better means of information than himself, but that their friends in that country were more hopeful than they had ever been. Lindsay's motion recommending recognition would be brought up in two days' time and an immense majority in the House of Commons favoured the South.

With a significant smile, the Emperor observed, "It is very singular that while you, Mr. Slidell, ask absolute recognition, the United States Minister, Mr. Dayton, is calling upon me to retract even my qualified recognition of you as belligerents!"

"That, your Majesty," was the retort, "is but further evidence of the insolence of the Washington Government."

Then Napoleon asked, assuming Anglo-French intervention, on what terms a peace could be made? The question of future boundaries, acceptable to both sides, was difficult if not insoluble. Slidell entered into

geographical explanations, but without a map it was
too puzzling. The Emperor apologised for not having
brought any maps to Vichy. However, Slidell attempted to make it clear, first, that reconstruction on
any terms was impossible (he lived to see that sinister
process in operation); second, that without European
intervention in some form any immediate peace was
impossible. Peace must be preceded by an armistice,
with Southern ports open to the commerce of the
world.

So the memorable interview drew to a close. The
Commissioner stated that he had prepared a formal
remand for recognition by the Emperor, which he
would present to Thouvenel, the Foreign Minister,
when the latter returned from London. His Majesty
said he saw no objection to this course and in parting
from Slidell expressed the hope that in future there
would be less difficulty in seeing him than hitherto.
As he gazed searchingly, perhaps quizzically, at his
visitor, it may be that their first meeting and Sophie
Bricard were in his thoughts.

Slidell returned to Paris highly pleased.

"I had been led to expect from what I had heard
of his habitual manner that he would be extremely
reserved, confining himself to asking questions, or
intimating on what points he wished me to speak,

with occasional brief observations on his part. On the contrary he was frank, unreserved, I might perhaps say, cordial; placing me entirely at my ease by the freedom with which he spoke himself. Although he said nothing to commit himself as to his future course, I left him with the decided impression that if England long persevered in obstinate inaction he would take the responsibility of moving by himself."

But would he? Did he dare? Upon the answer to that question the fate of the South hung.

CHAPTER IV

SLAVERY, COTTON AND CASH

ON the 9th October, 1862, George Eustis came into Slidell's room with a copy of the London *Morning Post* of the previous day. His expression was jubilant.

A speech of the English Chancellor of the Exchequer, Gladstone, at Newcastle, contained this passage, destined to an embarrassing immortality.

> "We know quite well that the people of the Northern States have not yet drunk of the cup—they are still striving to hold it far from their lips—which all the rest of the world see they must nevertheless drink of. We may have our opinions about slavery; we may be for or against the South; but there is no doubt that Jefferson Davis and other leaders of the South have made an army; they are making, it appears, a navy; and they have made what is more than either, they have made a nation!" (Loud and prolonged cheers.)

When Slidell had read it he arose, we are told, with flashing eyes and bringing his palm down upon his desk with a resonant thump, exclaimed, "If this means anything at all, it means immediate recognition!"

That very evening he sought the Comte de Persigny, who told him that the Emperor had already read Gladstone's speech and was convinced that the British Government was now committed and joint action by France and England must follow. Meanwhile his Majesty fully shared the British Minister's sentiments.

And in truth it seemed as if the moment had come at last. There were other occasions in the course of the next twelve months when it also seemed to have come —that long-awaited moment when both France and England would recognise the Confederate States of America. But if it ever came it could only come, with the fulfilment of a condition which, though regarded by their friends in Europe as vital, the Government at Richmond was still perversely indisposed to concede.

"We may have our opinion about slavery."

The prime motive, perhaps the original cause of Secession was slavery, the systematic subjection of the negro race in the South to vassalage, a system which had been condemned not only by European philanthropists, but by the most enlightened American slave-owners such as Washington and Jefferson themselves. Slavery, then, was no longer the real issue with the people of the South. It was only elsewhere that it continued to be the main issue.

> "Many of us remember," wrote a Southern Congressman to President Jefferson Davis in 1861, "when we heard slavery first declared to be the normal constitution of society; few will dare now to affirm it."

Sensible Southerners began asking themselves whether the institution was so vital to the prosperity of the cotton, sugar and tobacco plantations as they had supposed—whether the same labour would not be available under manumission as before—whether it were really true that the moment their shackles (to use a figure of speech) were struck off four millions of blacks would rise and murder their former masters or, supposing they did not go to that extent, whether they would forthwith cease work and plunge planters and plantations into ruin—whether, in point of fact, things would not go on in an industrial and commercial sense very much as before and as they went on elsewhere.

For the latter is exactly what happened and within

a dozen years from the conclusion of the Civil War seven million bales of cotton were picked, pressed and sold in the South, which was about double the quantity which had ever been produced before.

Nevertheless, slavery had undoubtedly been one prominent cause of the divergence, moral, economic and political, between the two sections of the country. It had changed, with the help of climate, the character and tastes of two peoples, just as the character of the English colonists in America had from other causes changed long prior to 1776.

But while slavery had been a cause, the extent of the cleavage was due to a desire for independence—for separate political powers and a social régime, to a conviction on the part of the South that they had no more and indeed a good deal less in common with the commercial and manufacturing North than New England had with Old England in 1776.

> "We have every reason," Slidell had said in a speech in the Senate in 1858, "to be a united and harmonious people; but we cannot shut our eyes to the melancholy fact that at this day there prevails between the masses of the people of the Eastern and Southern States as deep a feeling of alienation—I might say of animosity—as ever existed between England and France."

Lord Russell once pertinently expressed the wish that while the people of the North continued to celebrate their Declaration of Independence, they had "inculcated upon their own minds that they should not go to war with six millions of their fellow-countrymen who want to put the principles of 1776 into operation as regards themselves."

The statesmen of the North, and particularly Lincoln himself, made great play with the idea of the "sacredness" of the "Union, one and indivisible"—the "Union forever." It might have cheered the ghost of Alexander Hamilton; but the people of the twentieth century have grown sceptical and a little cynical about sacrificing their racial, national or even social entity on the altar of any mere federal unity. The Wilsonian gospel of national self-determination is not perhaps quite as popular as it was in 1919—yet we are rather inclined to sympathise with any community (or individual) whose will or whose tendencies are perpetually thwarted by an overbearing and incompatible partner, and in such cases the rational solution appears to be divorce. Union and partnership—other than by mutual consent—has grown to be obsolete in doctrine and practice—and the idea of taking up arms and shedding blood to force two equal and unsympathetic communities, commonwealths or individuals to dwell together in an artificial bond is no longer regarded as practical politics or even common wisdom.

To us of the twentieth century the tenacity, not to say bigotry, with which the North clung to the notion of a political and territorial integrity, which was not at all in the minds of the founders of their federation, and was in 1861 flatly rejected by no fewer than thirteen of the State governments composing that union, seems truly astonishing until we reflect how recently this was the British attitude towards Ireland and South Africa, and that it still persists in some quarters. But there is a distinction to be drawn between revolting dependencies and seceding free commonwealths. The Southern States were not vassals to the North; they were equal partners, as a later President, himself a Southerner, put it:

> "When they considered that the time had come to put their right of withdrawal from the Union into practice, the Southern statesmen showed at once, with a manifest naturalness and sincerity, what generation they were of. They acted, with an all but unconscious instinct, upon the principles of 1788, and they conceived the unmaking of the constitution to be not an act of revolution or of lawless change, but a simple, though it were solemn, legal transaction, like the formal abrogation of a great treaty, to be effected by the same means by which it had originally

been adopted.... There was no steadfast love for the Union in the South as in the North.... They were an English folk, strengthened here and there by the sober Scots-Irish strain and the earnest blood of the steadfast Huguenot. They held to their principles, their habits, their prepossessions with a simple, instinctive, undeliberate consistency.... It was by appealing to their very conservatism that the advocates of secession had won." *

That these people could be called "rebels," "traitors" and "insurgents" and heaped with every kind of insult and opprobrium which is usually reserved for criminals beyond the pale of the law, naturally shocked Europe. The only factor which gave any colour to the charge of moral obliquity was slavery, and the abuses of slavery were glaring. There were slave-owners like the notorious General Hampton who treated their black serfs almost as badly as millions of white serfs were treated in Russia, who sweated and ground them down even more heartlessly than the iron-masters and meat packers of a later generation did their white wage-slaves. But those abuses might have been corrected, as the major abuses of nineteenth century civilisation have been mitigated or altogether abolished. It was the idea, the principle, the name of slavery

* Woodrow Wilson: *A History of the American People.*

which was obnoxious to all except the small slave-holding class in the South numbering some ninety thousand people out of a population of six millions.

Slavery had then ceased to be the real issue in the South at an early stage in the conflict. Yet, from the moment when it repudiated Lincoln's offer of money compensation for the slave-owners, the South imagined that it would have to defend slavery, because to have accepted the offer would have meant political reunion with the North. The South did not want re-union. Henceforward they embarked on a wrong policy, because the Confederate Government could very well have given up the "peculiar institution" of slavery voluntarily. Emancipation might have angered the plantation oligarchy, it might have outraged the political fanatics; but emancipation would really have hurt nobody and it would have won the Confederacy its independence. For it was slavery and slavery alone which fed outraged Northern public opinion, inflamed Northern zeal and recruited the Northern armies. And it was slavery and slavery alone which prevented English and French peoples and their Governments time and time again from acknowledging the Confederate States as the nation which Gladstone declared it had become.

To us it seems astonishing that the South should

not have realised this as far as Europe was concerned. They should themselves have anticipated Lincoln's Proclamation and announced to the occupants of a million cabins that thereafter they would be free to work from dawn to sunset in return for their food, lodging and raiment, just as the farm and factory labourers in England, France, Germany and America itself did, and as the free blacks must also do, or else starve or emigrate. How many of the Southern plantation hands subsequently emigrated? How many did not, when hostilities had ceased and they were "free," look back with regret for life on the old terms, when it was worth the master's while to look after his workers, and to keep them healthy and happy?

The slave-owning class in the South told the mass of the people that emancipation would prove their economic ruin. They conjured up a picture of deserted cotton-fields and plantations gone to waste; but in their hearts what they actually dreaded most was the destruction of their own caste privileges and political predominance, the rise of a commercial and industrial class scornful of the quasi-feudal aristocracy which had been created south of the Mason and Dixon line. And these fears were justified. The special type of civilisation which characterised the Southern States has disappeared, but its disappearance is due to other causes than the mere change in the moral and economic relationship between master and labourer.

The irresistible forces making for the homogeneity of the American people, North and South—the melting-pot which fuses all classes and characteristics into one and obliterates original distinctions, these have been the potent agents of the social revolution. For the black helots not only still toil on the great plantations, but they have trebled in number. A recent visitor to the South seeing them pour forth in their thousands, labouring early and late with bent backs and sweating brows in the heat of the sun, notes their low wages, coarse food and crowded cabins, and exclaims: "So this—*this* is the dangerous freedom that the North gave the black man and the Confederacy perished rather than bestow!"

As the war progressed the clearest heads in the Confederacy came to realise that in cleaving to the institution of slavery they were giving fatal hostages to fortune. But hardly one amongst the leaders, from Jefferson Davis downwards, had the courage to advocate the liberating step. One man in particular was under no illusions, the man who was called "the brains of the Confederacy," Judah Philip Benjamin. But Benjamin was a soldier of fortune, the paid counsel of his masters; he knew well the sources and the limitations of his power. He had only to cast a single glance at that grim assembly of aged Senators and Representatives who had been sent or had sent themselves to the Confederate capital, for the most part peevish, domineering men, filled with pride, bigotry and intolerance. It was this crowd of eighteenth century planter-politicians at Richmond who really ruled the South, and who made bold, enlightened statesmanship almost impossible. The best men, the strong, sensible, heroic spirits of the South were away fighting, and one gathers to-day from their letters and diaries that they had no very exalted opinion of the way affairs were being managed by Jefferson Davis and the recalcitrant clique at the capital.

When the foregoing is considered one perceives why the great chance of jettisoning slavery was not taken until it was too late, in spite of the repeated warnings of Yancey, Slidell, Mason, Lamar, Spence and others. It was not taken because it was impossible, unless all this narrow-minded fanatical clique of lawyers, plantation-owners, and superannuated fire-eaters could have been swept away and a measure of emancipation courageously insisted and acted upon. The run of politicians in the South was singularly full of prejudices and arrogance, intolerant of outside criticism and utterly lacking in humour and a spirit of compromise.

They knew and cared nothing for foreign opinion. When Yancey and his colleagues came to Europe in 1861 and saw for themselves how slavery was regarded they recognised that they had under-rated the strength of abolitionist sentiment. A few weeks later they issued a joint manifesto declaring the Southern States fit and worthy in every respect for independence and added:

> "We are also aware that the anti-slavery sentiment, so universally prevalent in England, has shrunk from the idea of forming friendly public relations with a Government recognizing the slavery of a part of the human race. Nevertheless, the question of the morality of slavery it is not for the undersigned to discuss with any foreign Power."

That is what they had been told to say and under sharp admonitions from Richmond some of them continued to say it to the very end.

Yancey spent a year abroad and returned to the South in ill-health, a disappointed and disillusioned man. In a speech made in New Orleans to his supporters he told them that he had no "glad tiding from over the sea": that Queen Victoria and Prince Albert were against them.

> "Gladstone we can manage: but," he went on, "the feeling against slavery in England is so strong that

no public man there dares extend a hand to help us. We have got to fight the Washington Government alone. There is no government in Europe that dares help us in a struggle which can be suspected of having for its result, directly or indirectly, the fortification or perpetuation of slavery. Of that I am certain."

But the warning was wasted on Jefferson Davis and his friends who clung obstinately to their fatal prejudices.

On October 22, 1862, Slidell had another lengthy interview with Napoleon at St. Cloud.

"The Emperor," he wrote, "received me in the most friendly manner. Taking me by the hand, he inquired how I had been, and invited me to be seated. He then asked me what news I had from America, and how our affairs were going on. I replied that we were entirely cut off from the reception of any news, that we were obliged to take our intelligence from the Northern press, and that he well knew how little reliable it was, being subject to the most arbitrary surveillance over everything connected with the war. But in spite of that surveillance the truth could, after a certain lapse of time, be gleaned even from Northern journals, and especially from the private correspondence of persons at New York and elsewhere. Since I had the honour of seeing him at Vichy our position had most materially improved, and was now better than at any previous period. Our troops were as numerous and better disciplined than they had ever been; that time and opportunity had developed high military talent in many of our officers, while there was a singular absence of that quality among Northern generals; while we anxiously desired to see the war brought to a close, we had no apprehensions whatever of the final result of the contest; we had the immense advantage over our enemies of harmonious counsels and a thoroughly united people ready and willing to make every sacrifice, and submit to any privation for the establishment of their independence."

The Emperor replied that he was entirely satisfied of the correctness of all that Slidell had said; he had no scruple in declaring his sympathies were entirely with the South; his only desire was to know how to give them effect; the condition of affairs in Europe was very unsatisfactory; especially in Italy and Greece; he was obliged to act with great caution, and intimated that if he acted alone, England, instead of following his example, would endeavour to embroil him with the United States, and French commerce would be destroyed. He asked his visitor for his own views.

Slidell declared that he had no hope of any friendly action from England,

"until the time should arrive when it would become
a matter of indifference to us; all we asked for was
recognition, satisfied that the moral effect of such a
step, by giving confidence to the peace party at the
North, would exercise influence; if it had been
taken a few months since, it would have secured the
election of a majority of the House of Representatives opposed to the war. Recognition would not
afford, in the eyes of the world, the slightest pretext
for hostilities on the part of the North; there were,
however, stronger reasons that would bind them to
keep the peace—their mercantile tonnage was infi-
nitely larger than that of France, and that in the same
proportion would be their losses at sea; that their
navy, of which they boasted so loudly, would be
swept from the ocean, and all their principal ports
efficiently blockaded by a moiety of his powerful
marine, and that the *Gloire* or the *Normandie* could
enter without risk the harbours of New York and
Boston, and lay those cities under contribution. I told
him the condition of Fort Warren, manned by raw
militia; the ports of New York would not be better
defended, as they were only garrisoned by new levies,
who so soon as they had been drilled for a few weeks
were sent to the armies in the field and replaced by
fresh recruits; and, above all, the energies and resources of the North were already taxed to their
utmost by the war in which they were engaged, and
that mad and stupid as the Washington government

had shown itself to be, it still had sense enough not to seek a quarrel with the first power of the world.

"The Emperor then asked, 'What do you think of a joint mediation of France, England, and Russia? Would it, if proposed, be accepted by the two parties?' I replied, that some months since I would have said that the North would unhesitatingly reject it, but that now it would probably accept it; that I could not venture to say how it would be received at Richmond. I could only give him my individual opinion. I had no faith in England, and believed that Russia would lean strongly to the Northern side; that the mediation of the three Powers, where France could be outvoted, would not be acceptable; that we might, perhaps, with certain assurances, consent to the joint mediation of France and England, but *knowing, as I did, the Emperor's sentiments, I would gladly submit to his umpirage.*

" 'My own preference,' stated Napoleon, 'is for a proposition of an armistice of six months, with the Southern ports open to the commerce of the world; this would put a stop to the effusion of blood, and hostilities would, probably, never be resumed. We can urge it on the high ground of humanity and the interest of the whole civilized world; if it be refused by the North, it will afford good reason for recognition, and, perhaps, for more active intervention.' I said that such a course would be judicious and acceptable; indeed, it was one that I had suggested to

Mr. Thouvenel, when I first saw him in February last. I feared, however, he would find it as difficult to obtain the co-operation of England for it as for recognition. He said that he had reason to suppose the contrary; that he had a letter from the King of the Belgians which he would show me. He did so."

It was an autograph letter from King Leopold to the Emperor, dated Brussels, 15th October; the date was important, as Queen Victoria was then at Brussels. The King urged, in the warmest manner, for the cause of humanity and in the interests of the suffering populations of Europe, that prompt and strenuous efforts should be made by France, England and Russia to put an end to the bloody war that then desolated America. He expressed his perfect conviction that "all attempts to reconstruct the union of the United States are hopeless, that final separation is an accomplished fact, and that it is the duty of the great powers so to treat it; that recognition, or any other course that might be thought best calculated to bring about a peace, should be at once adopted. The appeal is made with great earnestness to the Emperor to bring the whole weight of his great name and authority to bear on the most important question of his day. It is universally believed that King Leopold's counsels have more influence with Queen Victoria

than those of any living man; that in this respect he
has inherited the succession of the late Prince Consort."

Slidell repeated to the Emperor what he had said
to Drouyn de Lhuys, of the assertions of Lord Cowley
and others, that no intimation of his wishes and views
on the question had been made to the British Government.

"He smiled and said that he supposed that it was
in accordance with diplomatic usages to consider
nothing to exist that had not been formally written;
that Thouvenel must have spoken to Cowley, and
intimated that *perhaps Mr. T. might not have endeavoured to impress Lord Cowley with the idea that he
was much in earnest.* I have had strong suspicion on
this score for some time past, and am inclined to
think that the feeling that Mr. Thouvenel did not
fairly represent his views on this, as well as on the
Italian question, may have had some influence on the
decision of the Emperor to dispense with the services
of Mr. Thouvenel as Minister of Foreign Affairs; it
is very certain that his resignation was invited by the
Emperor."

The Emperor went on to ask Slidell why the South
had not created a navy; and forthwith proceeded to
throw out a suggestion which was to have the most
important consequences. "He said," reported Slidell,

"that we ought to have one; that a few ships would have inflicted fatal injury on the Federal commerce, and that with three or four powerful steamers we could have opened some of our ports. I replied that at first many of our leading men thought it would be bad policy to attempt to become a naval power, as we had no good ports for large vessels but Norfolk and Pensacola, few seamen, and an inconsiderable mercantile marine; that we would always be essentially an agricultural people, selling freely to all the world and buying in the cheapest markets; we could rely on our peaceful disposition to preserve us from collisions with European powers, while at the same time it would be the interest of those powers to prevent our only probable enemies from abusing their superiority over us at sea; that we all now saw our error and were endeavouring to correct it, that we had built two vessels in England, and were now building others—two of which would be powerful iron-clad steamers; that the great difficulty was not to build, but to man and arm them, under the existing regulations for the preservation of neutrality; *that if the Emperor would give only some kind of verbal assurance that his police would not observe too closely when we wished to put on board guns and men, we would gladly avail ourselves of it.*

"He said, *'Why could you not have them built as for the Italian government? I do not think it would be difficult, but I will consult the Minister of Marine about it.'* "

King Leopold, in his letter, spoke of his wishes for the success of the French arms in Mexico, and the establishment under their protection of a stable and regular government. This gave Slidell an opportunity of alluding to the propositions he had made at Vichy, and to hold out the advantages which would result to France from a cordial and close alliance between the two countries, not so much depending on treaties and mere paper bonds as resulting from mutual interests and common sympathies.

"An idea prevails," wrote Slidell, "among some of the officers who have gone to Mexico, that as troops and ships have been sent there on a scale vastly greater than the apparent objects of the expedition require, that the Emperor has some ulterior views, perhaps to occupy the old French colony of St. Domingo, as Spain has done for the eastern portion of the island. *I took occasion to say to the Emperor that, however distasteful such a measure might be to the Washington Government, ours could have no objection to it.*"

While the question of recognition was on the *tapis,*

the Emperor said that he had seen a letter from a New York which he wished his visitor to read, to have his opinion of the correctness of the views it expressed. "It was a letter that I had previously seen—it being addressed to Mr. Lindsay, M.P., who consulted me about the propriety of placing it before the Emperor, as he had already done with Earl Russell. At my instance Mr. Lindsay handed it to Mr. Michel Chevalier, a senator standing high in the Emperor's confidence. The letter purported to be the expression of the opinion of many leading Democrats that recognition of the South would soon bring the war to a close. As the writer was well known to me as a man of high character and intelligence, I assured the Emperor that he might confidently rely on the fairness and accuracy of his statements. In the same connection the Emperor spoke of an article in a Richmond paper which had attracted his attention, and which he said had produced some impression on his mind. It was an article from the *Dispatch*, I think, and which has gone the rounds of most of the European papers, especially those friendly to the North. It deprecates recognition as tending only to irritate the people of the North, and to stimulate to increased exertion, while it would be of no service to the South. I have been more than once surprised to hear this article referred to in conversation by intelligent persons well-disposed towards our cause on whom it seemed also to have had some effect. I told the Emperor that there were at least five, perhaps more, daily papers published in Richmond, and that, if my recollections were correct, it was the one that had the least influence; that the article was but the expression of the individual opinion of an anonymous writer who, in all probability, if he were known, would prove to be a man without the slightest position, social or political." *

The conversation then turned upon the characters of Generals Lee, Johnston, and "Stonewall" Jackson, and Napoleon expressed his admiration of the recent march of Stuart's cavalry into Pennsylvania, crossing the Potomac at Hancock and recrossing below Harper's Ferry.

"He asked me to trace the route on the map, and was astonished at the boldness and success of the enterprise. He expressed his surprise at the large number of killed and wounded in various battles, and asked if the accounts were not exaggerated. I said that, so far as the enemy were concerned, they were, on the contrary, systematically very much understated; that as they had acknowledged a loss of more

* Nevertheless, this article was in all probability inspired by President Davis himself.

than fourteen thousand in the Maryland battles, there was every ground for believing that it was nearer twenty-five thousand. He remarked, 'Why, this is a frightful carnage; we had but twelve thousand *hors de combat* at Magenta.' 'But,' I replied, 'Solferino and Magenta produced decisive results, while with us successive victories do not appear to bring us any nearer to the termination of the war.'

"The whole interview was," concludes Slidell, "as well in manner as in substance, highly gratifying. On taking leave the Emperor again shook hands. I mention this fact, which would appear trivial to persons not familiar with European usages and manners, because it afforded additional evidence of the kindly feeling manifested in his conversation, which, by the way, was conducted entirely in English."

The Confederate Government had committed a further blunder at the very outset of hostilities. They had neglected to establish, early in 1861, mercantile relations with Europe, which would have been productive of a vast financial asset. If they had promptly laid hold of every ship of their own and given inducements to foreign shipping to transport a quarter of a million bales of cotton to England and France or to any European port, they would have provided themselves with a fund of ready money sadly needed to arm, clothe and equip the armies in the fields, months before their enemies were ready. For the cotton was there on their wharves, representing millions of dollars. The ports were still open. It only needed concentration, foresight and energy. Five months elapsed from the secession of South Carolina to the firing of the first shot, and in these five months little or nothing was done.

In their defence it has been urged that no general executive government existed, and even the Provisional Government of the first of the seceding States was not formed until February, 1861, and then was not strong enough to control action and public opinion in the States. The ships already loaded with cotton made haste to get away. But it was on account of private transactions and they did not return. In May, 1861, it was too late. A Federal blockade was declared and moving cotton became a risky, though enormously profitable, business. And hundreds of thousands of bales for which Europe was clamouring now remained piled up on the wharves.

Among the reputable banking houses in Paris during the Empire was the one of which Emil Erlanger, originally of Frankfort, was the head. It was the Comte de Persigny who brought Erlanger and Slidell together, but Erlanger had had previous relations with

Southern planters and cotton-brokers who had come
to Paris, and enjoyed a wide acquaintance amongst
leading members of the Southern colony in the capital.
His sympathies therefore were with the South, while,
on another count, he could not regard without interest
the prominent, not to say leading, position that a
member of the Jewish race was taking in Confederate
Councils. Another circumstance soon increased his
cordiality. The banker had a goodlooking son,
Frederic, of artistic talents, who meeting Miss Matilda Slidlel had fallen deeply in love with her. At
informal meetings, chiefly after-dinner talks, in the
Avenue d'Antin, the conversation of the elders once or
twice turned to the subject of Confederate finance.
One evening, in September, 1862, Erlanger *père*
observed that the cotton held in the South was excellent security for a loan if only the chances of moving
it improved. In any case, the European investing public might be inclined to regard it as a very promising
speculation. "In fact," pursued Erlanger, "I believe
several million pounds sterling might be raised on the
delivery of the cotton. My firm might be inclined, if
we can agree upon the terms, to carry through the
issue. Of course, if recognition occurs, or the blockade
were lifted, it would be an enormous success. But we
will take the risk."

Slidell was charmed with the proposal.

"I have been quite surprised," he wrote Mason (September 26), "at an uninvited suggestion on the part of a respectable banking house to open a credit to our Government of a considerable amount. No distinct proposition as to the terms or amount, but the basis to be cotton to be delivered to the parties making the advance at certain ports in the interior."

Slidell was almost tempted to take the entire responsibility of accepting the banker's proposal, but considering that the bulk of the money would probably come out of English pockets, he thought it safer to divulge the scheme to his colleague in London.

The Erlangers, he told Mason, were "one of the richest and most enterprising banking houses in Europe, having extensive business relations throughout France and free access to some very important men about the Court. They will, in anticipation of the acceptance of their propositions, actively exert themselves in our favour and enlist in the scheme persons who will be politically useful." He, therefore, approved of the scheme, subject to possible modifications. The terms proposed were a loan of £3,000,000 in 7 per cent bonds issued at 77, convertible into cotton at sixpence a pound to be delivered within six months after peace.

When they heard of the scheme, the Government at Richmond was by no means captivated by it. Particularly did they object to the price at which the loan was to be offered and to Erlanger & Co.'s commission. Although they did not withhold their sanction, they so far doubted Slidell and Mason's ability to embark on high financial enterprise that they proceeded to appoint a special Treasury agent, Brigadier General Colin McRae, to check and control all Confederate money dealings in Europe. But before this person appeared on the scene the prospectus of the Cotton Loan had been drawn up and issued. As it turned out Slidell never ceased to regret the smallness of the amount of the loan which was decided upon. This regret, it may be mentioned, was not shared later by the English and French investors.

On March 4, 1863, Slidell wrote to Benjamin:

"In my conversation with M. Drouyn de Lhuys, I mentioned the loan of Erlanger & Co. and invoked his good offices in carrying it out, saying that these gentlemen considered it important that it should be advertised in the Paris papers, but that the advertisement could not be made without the assent of the Government. He expressed his wishes for the success of the loan, but thought that he could not consent to the advertisement; that the object could be

equally well attained by circular, etc., while adver-
tisements would excite unfriendly comment and
probably be made the subject of a protest from the
Federal Minister.

"The consent of the Minister of Finance, M. Fould,
had been obtained, subject however to the approbation of the Minister of Foreign Affairs. Erlanger &
Co. then brought the subject before the Emperor,
who very promptly directed his secretary to write a
note to the Minister requesting him to grant an audience to M. Erlanger on an urgent matter in which
he felt great interest.

"The result of the audience was the withdrawal
by M. Drouyn de Lhuys of his objections, and the
loan will now be simultaneously advertised here
and in London. I mention this fact as offering renewed evidence of the friendly feeling of the Emperor."

When issued the prospectus attracted instant and
widespread attention. The offices of Oppenheimer and
Co. in London were besieged by intending investors,
and for days the brokers were inundated by orders for
the Confederate Cotton bonds which were issued at
90 per cent of their gross value. A deposit of 15 per
cent was paid on allotment. The issue was subscribed
five times over, among the names of subscribers (for
£2000) being that of the Right Hon. W. E. Glad-

stone. In France, both the Duc de Morny and the Comte de Persigny applied for the bonds.

As the fortunes of the Cotton Loan were so intimately bound up with the Federal blockade, Slidell thought it time to take up this matter again with the French Government.

> "I shall not," he wrote Mason, "make it matter of formal communication, but will endeavour to induce this government to reconsider the whole question of blockade. All here admit that a gross error has been committed in recognising the efficiency of the blockade and only desire to find some plausible pretext for retracing the false steps. The evidence of the repeated intermissions of the blockade at many points and for several days which I presented was conclusive; the voluntary relaxation of the blockade offered in my opinion much stronger grounds for declaring it inefficient than its temporary suspension from *force-majeure*." *

But the Minister pointed out that France was already too far committed to recognition of the blockade for any withdrawal without the co-operation of England, and so could do nothing until a general change of attitude occurred.

Such a *laissez faire* policy could hardly fail to react

* February 19, 1863.

on the prosperity of the new loan. At first, its success had astonished the Federal authorities and their financial agents in London; but they quickly rallied all their forces with a view to discrediting the bonds. Already these had declined three or four points and Spence, who, until McRae's arrival, was acting as Confederate financial agent, dreaded a heavy further fall, before settling day, which might frighten off subscribers before they had paid the next instalment on the bonds. When Slidell's opinion was asked for he replied (April 5):

> "I do not see at present any sufficient motive for buying on account of our government; but the time may arrive before the settling day when it may be a good policy to do so. In the meanwhile, I think it would be well to agree that the amount of the loan should be reduced to two millions with the privilege however of taking the other million within some fixed delay. This would leave very little floating scrip for the operators for a fall to work on."

If sales went badly the Erlangers had the option of withdrawing from the whole transaction by paying a forfeit of £300,000 to the Confederacy. In Slidell's opinion, however, this was improbable.

> "I have no idea under any circumstances they will take this ground, for they would be very heavy losers,

having, as they inform me, expended large sums in conciliating certain interests and influences."

On March 30 the loan stood with apparent firmness at from 1¾ to 2 per cent premium and with every prospect of not falling below par. Then came a drop of several points which alarmed Mason. The Easter holidays offered a brief respite.

"At this time," reported Mason, "the Erlangers with their advisers in London came to me and represented that it was very manifest that agents of the Federal Government here and those connected with them by sympathy and interest were making concerted movements covertly to discredit the loan, by large purchases at low rates, and this succeeding to some extent had thus invited the formation of a 'bear' party, whose operations, if unchecked by an exhibition of confidence strongly displayed, might and probably would bring down the stock before settlement day (24th April) to such low rates as would alarm holders, and might in the end lead a large portion of them to abandon their subscriptions by a forfeiture of the instalments (15 per cent) so far paid. They said that they with their friends, with a view to sustain the market, had purchased as far as they could go; but unless a strong and determined power was interposed they could not be responsible for the panic that might arise, and they advised that I should give them authority to purchase on Government account, if necessary, to the extent of one million (sterling) at such times as might appear judicious, and until par was obtained.

"I represented the condition of things to Mr. Slidell and asked his counsel in the matter. He agreed with me that if necessary to prevent such serious consequences as might ensue to the Government credit, the proposed interposition should be made. I further requested Mr. Spence (who was kept fully cognizant of the condition of things) to confer with the depositaries (Trenholm & Co.) at Liverpool as to the projected measure, and to come up to London. He did so; and under these joint counsels, including Erlanger & Co., it was determined if the market opened after the Easter recess under the same depression, that the Government should buy through Erlanger & Co., but of course without disclosing the real party in the market, in the manner indicated. I enclose herewith a copy of the Articles of Agreement entered into with Erlanger & Co. to effect this end, dated on the 7th instant.

"The next day (the 8th) was the first business day after the holidays. The loan opened under great depression, and with declining tendencies. In the course of the day purchases were made for our account, at from 4 to 3 and 2½ discount to the amount of 100,000 pounds. This had the effect of bringing the rates at the close of the day to the point last named (2½ discount). The following day (yesterday), to use the language of the Stock Exchange, the 'bears' again made a rush, but were met by so decided a front, that at the close of the day the stock stood at ½ per cent premium, and it was said by our bankers (who report to me every morning) that there were strange manifestations of the bears creeping in at the close of the day, to cover themselves as well as they could, at rates ranging from ⅛ to ½ premium. Yesterday the amount purchased under the arrangement is reputed at about 300,000 pounds and our bankers believe that our work is substantially done, and that the stock will now gradually rise to a healthy condition, and a premium. Of course no purchase will be made above par. The operations of yesterday were chiefly at par. All this thing is of course done in confidence and silence. Should the market admit, or when it admits, sales will be made (never under par) until what the government may have bought shall be again placed. At worst, should it be found necessary to purchase to the extent proposed (of 1,000,000) the effect will only be, to reduce the loan by that amount.

"It is believed that after the adjustments ensuing at settlement day, and the payment of the next instalment of 10 per cent on the 1st of May, matters will become sufficiently permanent not only to dispense with further purchases but to enable us gradually to sell out.

"I hope you will see the necessity which called on

me to exercise this responsibility, and that what I
have done will have the approval of the Government.
I confess I was at first impression exceedingly averse
to it, and so expressed myself to Mr. Slidell, but
each day since I am better satisfied with what has
been done."

For a statesman with no previous knowledge of
Capel Court finance Mason was showing himself an
apt pupil.

The stratagem proved successful, but to maintain
the stock at a premium, such large purchases had to
be made that on April 24, a million sterling had been
expended. Next day was settlement day and as matters
still looked ominous Mason and Spence resolved if
necessary to buy half a million pounds more.

> "On the 25th the account between buyers and
> sellers was fully adjusted, and under circumstances
> leading to the belief that the 'bears' were sufficiently
> punished to make them cautious of future like
> attacks.
> "Mr. Spence, under whose advice and guidance I
> acted in this matter, remained in London during the
> operation, and was each day in the city, during busi-
> ness hours, attending to it in person. Both he and the
> bankers entertain strong hope, as the great mass of
> the stock is now in *certain* hands, that it will sustain
> itself on a level at least at *par,* or free from fluctua-

tions caused by its adversaries, and that it will have the benefit of an upward tendency by accounts favourable to the success of the Confederate arms, as they successively reach here.

"I shall not close this despatch for some days, and will have it in my power to note what effect may have been produced by the great and gratifying intelligence received yesterday of the signal repulse of the ironclads at Charleston, the abandonment of the attack on Vicksburg, and the dangerous position of the enemy's forces at Wilmington, N. C.

"The very large purchases that were required to sustain the stock afford the best evidence that without them it would have fallen so far below *par,* as to have brought it into great discredit, very possibly producing a panic, of fifteen per cent, rather than incur risk of greater loss: and the more I have thought on the subject the better I am satisfied of the correctness of our judgment in going to the market to sustain it. The next instalment is due on the 1st of May, which when paid, will amount to twenty-five per cent. After that, both the bankers and Mr. Spence are sanguine, that under favourable accounts from the South, the stock will so rapidly improve as to enable them, gradually, to *replace* what was bought in, by sales, from time to time, as the market would bear."

It was a risky business, but it succeeded. There was a "spurt" in Confederate bonds and they actually rose

Miss Matilda Slidell
(The late Baroness d' Erlanger)

to a premium five per cent above issuing price and for several months they were quoted at a higher figure than United States bonds.

Spence claimed a great part of the credit, and putting Slidell and the Erlangers aside, proceeded to negotiate with Oppenheimer & Co. for another Confederate loan—this time for £20,000,000, and on better terms. But this project was still-born. When Slidell was asked about the truth of this he denied it: to issue another loan so soon would be to injure the first loan irreparably. Besides, he disliked and distrusted Spence. "I have no faith in his judgment or business qualities," he wrote.

What Spence did not dream of was the close intimacy of Slidell with Erlanger, whose son a few weeks later led Miss Matilda Slidell to the altar. No wonder that both Slidell and Erlanger were angry. No wonder that the former wrote (May 15) that

> "Spence appears to consider that the powers of Secretary of the Navy as well as of the Treasury are vested in him. I am getting heartily tired of his meddling."

The success of the Confederate loan seems to have made its due impression on the Emperor who showed himself exceptionally cordial towards Slidell. An evi-

dence of this is seen in his sending him a copy of a
telegram which Minister Adams in London had despatched to Dayton in Paris, advising him that the Confederate *Japan,* alias *Virginia,* would probably enter
the French port of St. Malo. All foreign diplomatic
telegrams being regularly inspected by the Emperor's
secret police, Slidell was grateful for the tip and called
on his friend Mocquard to ask his advice as to what
action ought to be taken.

> "I said that of course I wished that every needful
> facility should be afforded by the Government for
> the repair of the steamer. He advised me to prepare a
> note to that effect which he would present to the
> Emperor and to feel reassured that all would be
> right."

Here was a small triumph for Slidell: for in this
instance he had certainly scored an advantage over
his diplomatic enemy, Dayton.

CHAPTER V

ARMAN AND HIS IRONCLADS

CONTRARY to the views held at Richmond at the outset of the war, Slidell had perceived that there was a far better chance of building Confederate cruisers in France than on the English side of the channel. He was confirmed in this opinion after his interview with the Emperor.

True, Napoleon III's Proclamation of Neutrality of June 10th, 1861, had closely followed that of her Britannic Majesty; in it the prohibitions were even more emphatically expressed. Instead of a formal enumeration of what was illegal, with a warning to French subjects against transgression, five clauses set forth the precise and specific acts which were forbidden. It was the third clause which was important:

"Il est interdit à tout Français de prendre commission de l'une des deux parties pour armer des vaisseaux en guerre, ou d'accepter des lettres de marque

pour faire la course maritime, ou de concourir d'une
manière quelconque à l'equipement ou l'armament
d'un navire de guerre ou corsaire de l'une des deux
parties."

This was explicit enough, and seemed therefore
final. But constitutional conditions in the two countries were not identical. France was governed by an
autocracy and no matter what enactments were made
or policy proclaimed, these could be modified or even
disregarded in practice without causing any public excitement or public or legal protest. As soon as Slidell
grasped this he, as early as October, 1862, wrote Captain Bulloch, the Confederacy's naval agent in England, that if he were to make arrangements to build
war vessels in France, it was improbable that the
builders would be interfered with or that the vessels
when completed would be unable to leave the French
ports, if a plausible pretext were offered. But at that
moment Bulloch was deeply committed to the Lairds,
English shipbuilders who having built the *Alabama*
and the *Florida,* were building four other vessels tech-
nically known as "rams" to his order, which the Federal authorities were determined should never stir
from their docks, if they could help it.

When the prospects of the Cotton Loan were at
their brightest, Slidell thought the time ripe for ac-

tion. He had made the acquaintance through Erlanger, of one Arman, a shipbuilder and naval
architect whose shipyards were at Bordeaux. Arman
was an important person; a member of the Legislative Council and on friendly terms with the Emperor.
His sympathies were with the Confederacy and he
expressed his readiness to undertake to build such
ships as were required. Another deputy, a notable
engineer and iron-founder, Voruz of Nantes, was
brought into the conference. Only two things were
now necessary: a formal assurance from Napoleon's
Minister of Marine, the Marquis de Chasseloup-Loubat (who had married a niece of the Confederate
General Beaurégard), that such ships when built
should be permitted to arm and proceed to sea, and
this Arman promised would be forthcoming.

Slidell now wrote Captain Bulloch, telling him of
the new prospect which had just been opened. Bulloch
was doubly worried in England. The financial commitments of the Confederacy were already so large as
to exhaust all his credit, and although the bankers,
Fraser, Trenholm and Co., supported him loyally, his
liabilities were increasing. Slidell urged Bulloch to
come to Paris and "try the French dockyards as soon
as the finances would admit of fresh operations, instead of depending upon the wavering policy of the

British Ministry and the probable delay, expense and publicity of a lawsuit."

The Loan was floated and Bulloch crossed the channel. He went to Bordeaux and contracted with Arman for four clipper corvettes of about 1,500 tons and four-hundred horse power, to be armed with twelve or fourteen six-inch rifled guns which was the *canon rayé de trente* of the French navy. As the utmost expedition was required the contract was split up equally between Arman and Voruz, the latter of whom got a local shipbuilder at Nantes to put up the hulls, which his own workmen completed, and fitted with guns and gear.

At the same time, Bulloch gave orders for two iron-clad ships of war suitable for entering the Mississippi. The Confederate Congress, anticipating the Loan, had appropriated £2,000,000 for such a purpose, hoping that such vessels might be purchased ready-built from the French navy. Slidell demonstrated the extreme unlikelihood of this. He did

"not see how the negotiation could be opened in such a way as to get the proposition before the Emperor unless it should appear that he had determined to recognise the Confederate Government independently of England," and there was "no evidence that he intended to take such a decisive step alone."

Under the circumstances, therefore, Bulloch would have to be "content with the covert intimation that no shipbuilder we might employ would be prevented from despatching the vessels to sea when they were completed."

Bulloch agreed and wrote Mallory, his official chief at Richmond:

> "You may rely upon it that the purchase of men-of-war from any of the European navies is not practicable under existing circumstances. The transaction would necessarily be managed through intermediaries, who, from the very nature of the negotiations, would be forced to sacrifice principle by prevaricating, and then all sorts of objectionable means would have to be used, even bribery, and after all we would only get cast-off vessels. I make these remarks as the result of experience, for I have had propositions from many persons, and I know wherein they are all wanting."

On June 1, 1863, Arman made his promised formal application to the Minister of Marine, in a document whose disingenuousness was perhaps demanded by the delicacy of the situation. It may be translated thus:

> "Bordeaux, June 1, 1863
>
> "Mr. Minister:
> "I request of your Excellency authority (in accordance with the Royal ordinance of July 12, 1847) to

equip with an armament of from twelve to fourteen thirty-pounders four steamships, now constructing, of wood and iron.

　·　　·　　·　　·　　·　　·　　·

"These ships are destined by a foreign shipper to ply the Chinese and Pacific seas, between China, Japan and San Francisco.

"Their specific armament contemplates their eventual sale to the governments of China and Japan.

"The construction of these ships has been in progress since the 15th of April last. I beg your Excellency will be good enough to accord to M. Voruz, as early as possible, the authorisation which I ask, as prescribed by the Royal ordinance of July 12, 1847.

　　　　　　　　　　　　　　"ARMAN."

To this the following response was received:

　　　　　　　　　　"Ministère de la Marine,
　　　　　　　　　　　"Paris, le 6 Juin, 1863.

"MONSIEUR,

"Je m'empresse de vous faire connaitre, en response à votre letter du 1er de ce mois, que je vous autorise volontiers à pouvoir d'un armement de douze à quatorze canons de trente les quatre batiments à vapeur en bois et en fer qui se construisent en ce moment à Bordeaux et à Nantes.

"Je vous prie de vouloir bien m'informer en temps utile de l'epoque à laquelle ces navires seront prets à prendre la mer afin que je donne les instructions

necessaires à MM. les chefs du service de la Marine
dans ces deux ports.

"Recevez, Monsieur, l'assurance de ma haute con-
sidération,

"Le Ministre Secretaire d'Etat de la Marine
et des Colonies,

"CHASSELOUP-LAUBAT." *

No wonder Bulloch heaved a sigh of relief. All went
well throughout the summer of 1863 with the construction of the four corvettes and the two ironclads
at Bordeaux and Nantes.

September came and still no suspicion was anywhere expressed concerning these vessels. Neither
Dayton, the American Minister, nor Consul-General
Bigelow had any knowledge of a covert encouragement to build them. Even if the truth of their ownership should be suspected and an official enquiry made
Slidell believed that Drouyn de Lhuys would reply

* "Ministry of Marine
"Paris, June 6, 1863
"SIR,
"I hasten to advise you in reply to your letter of the 1st instant
that I willingly authorise you to equip with an armament of twelve
thirty-pound guns the four steamships now constructing of wood
and iron at Bordeaux and Nantes. I will thank you to inform me
in time when the ships will be ready for sea, that I may give the
necessary instructions to the heads of the departments in these two
ports,

"CHASSELOUP-LAUBAT."

that Arman and Voruz were building the vessels in the ordinary course of business, as a purely commercial transaction, intending to despatch them for delivery abroad. Such was not contrary to French law and the Government could not interfere with the legitimate trade of the country.

But how earnestly Slidell, Bulloch, Arman and all the parties to the transaction hoped that the ships would be got off the stocks to sea before the secret of their ownership and destination leaked out!

Unhappily, such hopes were now to be shattered. It so chanced that Voruz had in his employ at Nantes a confidential clerk, an Alsatian, named Petermann. This man had a nephew in the shipping business who had been to America and had friends there. He was also a strong partisan of the North. One day an American marine had told him that if the South only had two or three warships they would blow Boston, New York and Philadelphia to atoms. Luckily for the North, England and France had forbidden the building of such ships and all attempts to do so in England had been discovered and foiled. The United States Government offered splendid rewards for information concerning attempted Confederate shipbuilding in English shipyards; they would probably do the same with regard to those in France.

All this made a deep impression on Petermann. For he was daily handling correspondence between his employer and the Confederate agents proving indubitably that the vessels now building both at Nantes and Bordeaux were for the Confederacy. This file of letters in his keeping also showed the complicity of the Government of his own country. But Petermann reflected that it was monstrous for France to give any support or encouragement to the upholders of slavery. He also allowed himself to wonder what price the American Minister in Paris would pay for copies of this compromising correspondence. When the confidential clerk had settled matters with his conscience he furtively made copies of all the letters in his employer's safe. Certain items which he remembered to have seen were at Arman's in Bordeaux: but it was easy enough to compose abstracts from memory. One or two he gratuitously invented to strengthen the case. On the 9th of September, pleading illness, he requested a few days' leave and took the train to Paris.

In Paris, Petermann went straight to the United States Legation, in Dayton's apartment at the Etoile. He asked to see the Minister, but the man's manner was so strange and suspicious that the Secretary, Pennington, kept close to his chief throughout the interview.

It gradually emerged that the caller had important information which he wished to sell to the United States Government. As this sort of business was being dealt with by Consul-General Bigelow, the mysterious Frenchman was referred to this official, in the Chaussée d'Antin.

What happened there the next morning is thus circumstantially narrated by Bigelow:

"A man of middle age presently entered, and after closing the door carefully and satisfying himself that we were alone, proceeded to say that he had a communication to make of considerable importance to my Government.

"I asked him to be seated and waited for him to proceed. He asked if I was aware that the Confederates were building war vessels in France? I replied that rumours of the kind had reached me, but as they came from or through wholly irresponsible sources, usually needy Confederate refugees, and had received no confirmation from our consuls at the ship-building ports, I had ceased to attach much importance to them. He proceeded to state as facts within his own knowledge that there were then building in the ports of Bordeaux and Nantes for account of the Confederate States of America several vessels, some of which were armour-plated and rams, which, together were to cost from twelve to fifteen millions of francs; that the engines for some of them were built and ready to be put in, that for the armament of these vessels artillery and shells had also been ordered. I remarked that no vessel of war could be built in France unless the official authorisation for the construction, equipment and arming of these vessels had already been issued from the Department of the Marine. I asked him if he meant seriously to affirm that the vessels he spoke of were building under an official authorisation of the government. He reaffirmed his statement, and added further that he was prepared to prove it to my entire satisfaction."

Bigelow says he tried not to betray his sense of the supreme importance of this communication, which was too circumstantial and precise to be wholly imaginary, if possibly exaggerated.

"Besides," he goes on to say, "I had attached more importance than any one else seemed to, to rumours of the same nature which had reached me previously, simply for the reason that the difficulties which the Confederates had encountered in their efforts to recruit their navy in England made it seem not only natural but almost inevitable that they should transfer their preparations to a country the government of which was supposed to be in greater sympathy with their schemes and where under such circumstances courts of justice would have less power to annoy.

"I said to my visitor: 'Of course what you state is

of grave importance to my Government if it can be substantiated, but of none at all without proofs which cannot be disputed or explained away. What kind of proofs can you furnish?' I asked.

" 'Original documents,' he said; 'and, what is more, I will engage that, with my proofs in hand, you can effectually secure the arrest of the ships.' "

But as the contractors, according to Petermann's statement, had already received an official authorisation from the Department of Marine to execute their contract for the Confederates, Bigelow asked him why he supposed any proofs he might produce could change the destiny of the ships? He replied that the official authorisation appeared on its face to have been procured through false representations.

Petermann thereupon produced a certified copy of the government authorisation and some half-dozen original letters and papers, testifying to the substantial truth of his statements.

"These papers he proposed to leave with me and to wait upon me again on the Saturday following, the interval to be employed by him in procuring some supplementary proofs which he described to me. I could no longer resist the conclusion that my visitor was in earnest, and that he was in possession of, or controlled, evidence of which no time should be lost in securing possession. Before he left I asked him upon what conditions I was to receive this service at his hands, for there was not much ground for presuming that his zeal for our national unity was entirely disinterested. He said that of course the papers were not obtainable without some expense and much trouble, and that when the documents he proposed to furnish me had actually defeated the naval operations of the Confederates in France, he would expect 20,000 francs. I replied to him that that was a large sum of money, but that I could not say that it was too large until I had seen what he proposed to bring me as its equivalent. If, however, I decided to use the papers, he might rely upon being properly compensated."

Finally, Petermann agreed to accept fifteen thousand francs and, having returned two days later with his *dossier,* the bargain, with Minister Dayton's approval, was concluded.

Bigelow now felt that he held in his hands all the proofs necessary to change the destination of the ships, "four of which at least threatened to be more formidable on the high seas than any ship in our navy and each of which I supposed to be capable of entering the harbour of New York and of laying the vast wealth of our commercial metropolis under contribution with comparative impunity."

He therefore sent the incriminating documents to Dayton, who promptly took them to the French Foreign Minister, Drouyn de Lhuys.

The Minister was "surprised and vexed" at such a disclosure; he recognised the hand of the Emperor. He did not believe that Chasseloup-Loubat would have signed such an authorisation except under pressure from higher quarters.

Clearly, this was a case for extreme caution and he therefore requested time to consider what should be done.

On the very next day Commissioner Slidell was in possession of the facts of Petermann's betrayal. He telegraphed Bulloch to come and see him. On his arrival Slidell told him: "We are in trouble about the ships. Dayton and his spies have corrupted one of Voruz's clerks who has supplied him with copies of all our correspondence. This has been shown officially to the Government by Dayton who demands an enquiry."

"But, surely," protested Bulloch, "the Government itself authorised the building."

"No; it was the Minister of Marine, at the direct request of the Emperor—quite a different thing. Drouyn de Lhuys may now disavow the whole transaction. Arman has been sent for and is coming to see me after he has had an interview with the Emperor. I felt you ought to be warned." *

Weeks elapsed; and although nothing definite occurred the rumours were current in Paris and London concerning certain warships being built at Bordeaux and Nantes for the Confederates. Bulloch, reporting what had happened to his chief at Richmond, wrote (Nov. 26, 1863):

"The builders are still sanguine that they will be allowed to send their ships to sea, but I confess that I do not see any such assurance in what they say, and the manner in which the protest of the American Minister has been received is well calculated to confirm my doubts. When Mr. Dayton went to the Minister of Foreign Affairs with a complaint and with copies of certain letters to substantiate it, the Minister might have said, 'These are alleged copies of the private correspondence of two prominent and highly respected French citizens; they could only have come into your possession by means of bribery or treachery. I cannot, therefore, receive them as evidence, and must insist that you produce the originals and explain how you came to be possessed of them.' It strikes me that such a course would have effectually silenced Mr. Dayton, and we could have felt some assurance of getting our ships to sea. Instead of this,

* Eustis Papers.

the stolen letters have been received without hesitation, and the United States officials profess to be satisfied with the action, or promised action, of the French Government. The builders are sent for, and warned by the Minister of Marine, and although those gentlemen come from their interviews still possessed by the belief that the ships will be allowed to depart, and thus, as I said before, excite hopes, I cannot be blind to the significancy of the above circumstances....

"If at the time our cause is in the ascendent, the local authorities will be instructed not to be too inquisitive, and the departure of our ships will be connived at. If, on the contrary, the Federal cause prospers, the affair of the 'Confederate ships' will be turned over to the responsible Ministers of the Empire, who will justify their claim to American gratitude by a strict enforcement of the neutrality of France. Hoping always for the best, I shall not permit any fears to create delay in the progress of the work. The ships shall be ready as soon as possible, and every effort shall be made to get them to sea in the manner least calculated to compromise the French authorities, if they choose only to be judiciously blind."

On the whole Bulloch thought that construction would not be interfered with, but whether the ships would be allowed to leave France or not "will depend upon the position of affairs in America at the time of their completion."

So matters went on until February, 1864, when the long-dreaded blow fell. Arman and Voruz were formally notified that the ironclads could not be permitted to sail and that the corvettes must not be armed in France, but must be sold nominally to some foreign merchant and despatched as ordinary trading vessels.

It was a bitter disappointment.

To the conference between Slidell and Bulloch, Captain Barron was called in to consider what was now to be done. The proposition of Arman that a nominal sale of the corvettes should be made to a Danish banker and that there should be a private agreement providing for a re-delivery to the Confederate agent at some foreign port was rejected. If a similar stratagem in the case of the English ships had failed, what hope of success would there be for the Danish man of straw?

It was decided to sell the ironclads. As the four corvettes were originally intended to act in conjunction with the ironclads in raising the Southern blockades and that object being no longer practicable, both the naval men, Bulloch and Barrow, were disposed to sell the corvettes also, or at least two of them. But to this Slidell would not agree:

"Should we withdraw our cruisers," he said, "the Federal flag would resume on the ocean the rank which we have forced it to abdicate. We cannot expect the *Alabama* and *Florida* always to avoid the pursuit of the enemy and we should be prepared to supply their loss. The *Rappahannock* may prove as unfit for that service as the *Georgia* and make only a single cruise."

He continued:

"A few months may produce great changes in our favour. I know that the Emperor's feelings are as friendly as ever, and a new Ministry in England may enable him to indulge them; the chapter of accidents is always in the long run fruitful of great and unexpected results. Perhaps it may be better to go on and complete the ships; there is no reason to apprehend any interruption in the work, and there is no danger whatever of losing them by any proceedings similar to those pending in England, as there is no municipal law prohibiting the fitting out of ships of war for the belligerent powers with whom France is at peace."

So it was agreed to push on the work on the corvettes as fast as possible, but to proceed with the ironclads more leisurely, while considering what could eventually be done with them.

At last the month of June, 1864, arrived and with it "the most remarkable and astounding circumstance that has yet occurred to our operations in Europe."

When the consultations had been held in Slidell's office in February it was agreed that the vessels must be sold, but that the sale of the corvettes should be purely fictitious. In May Arman showed Bulloch and Slidell's secretary, Eustis, a contract of sale of one of the ironclads to Denmark, which would probably also take the other. As this country was then at war, the Swedish Government consented to take over the rams on behalf of its neighbour. Arman agreed to deliver the vessels at Gottenberg in Sweden. He had made this arrangement in order that he might be able to send the ships to sea under the French flag and in charge of his own crew.

"Now," explained Arman, "if you are willing to sacrifice one of the rams, and will consent to the *bonafide* delivery of the first one, I am sure that the second can be saved to you. When the first ram is ready to sail," he continued, "the American Minister will no doubt ask the Swedish Minister if the vessel belongs to his Government. The reply will be 'yes'; she will sail unmolested, and will arrive at her destination according to contract. This will avert all suspicion from the second ram, and when she sails under like circumstances with the first, my people, having a previous understanding with you, will take her to any rendezvous that may have been agreed upon, or will deliver her to you or your agent at sea."

Slidell and Bulloch agreed to this. Bulloch proposed his friend, Captain Tessier, for the job of managing the whole business, but impressed upon M. Arman that they must have assurance that when they were ready to move, the Government would permit the vessels to leave. Arman replied that there was no doubt in his mind that the corvettes could steam out if unarmed; but that he was to have a personal interview with the Emperor within a fortnight which he hoped would allay all fears.

One evening Captain Tessier was seated with some of his seafaring companions at their rendezvous in Paris, when a message was delivered from M. Arman asking him to meet him at once at the Grand Hotel. There he found the shipbuilder and deputy in a state of great perturbation.

"It is all over," he said, mopping his brow. "I have tried to find Mr. Slidell, but he is out of Paris, and Captain Bulloch has gone to Liverpool. Tomorrow the rams and the corvettes must be sold—*tomorrow!* And it must be a bona fide sale, or our Government will have them seized and taken to Rochefort."

Arman told of his stormy reception by the Emperor. He had been rated severely and even threatened with imprisonment. Orders would be issued of the most peremptory kind not only directing the sale, but requiring absolute proof of its genuineness, and the next day Arman would receive these orders in writing from the Minister of Marine. Captain Bulloch must therefore realise the situation; Arman must wash his hands of the whole affair. One of the rams and two corvettes had been offered to Prussia, the second ram to Denmark and the two Nantes corvettes to Peru. These offers had been accepted.

If Slidell was "both astonished and indignant," his astonishment and indignation were less than Bulloch's.

> "My first impulse was to resist and to take legal proceedings to prevent the transfer of the ships to the purchasers. But a moment's reflection satisfied me that such a course could not be reclaimed for use during the war. The proclamation of neutrality issued by the Emperor of the French on the 10th of June, 1861, contained a specific prohibition against any aid whatever being given by a French subject to either belligerent, and if the Government had determined to enforce that prohibition strictly and literally, no effective resistance could be offered, and no plausible evasion could be attempted."

Back again in Paris, Bulloch and Arman met at Slidell's office in the rue Marignan. There they read the letter from Chasseloup-Loubat. Its duplicity shocked Bulloch, who wrote to Mallory that he had imagined that "this kind of crooked diplomacy had died out since the last century and would not be ventured upon in these common-sense days." The Minister wrote in a style of virtuous indignation; specified the character of the ships in detail as if he had made a startling discovery. Why, he exclaims, these offences are monstrous! And yet this was the same Marquis de Chasseloup-Loubat who on June 6 in the previous year had signed a formal authorisation to arm these very ships with fourteen heavy guns each!

Still it was useless to cry over spilt milk; they must hasten to recoup themselves as best they could for the great financial outlay. It was an added bitterness that the ships had been sold with the Emperor's approval to Prussia at a moment when that country was actually at war with Denmark.

But, as we shall see, Slidell and Bulloch had not really heard the last of Monsieur Arman and his ironclads.

Slidell's despatch concerning the clerical traitor at Nantes roused Judah R. Benjamin to cold fury.

"I am not at all surprised," he wrote (January 8, 1864), "at the accounts you give of the action of the Northern emissaries in suborning perjury, committing thefts and forging documents, for the furtherance of their objects. No crime is too revolting for this vile race, which disgraces civilization and causes one to blush for our common humanity. You have been removed from the scenes of their outrages, and are evidently startled at conduct on their part which we look for as quite naturally to be expected. A people who have been engaged for the three last years in forging our Treasury notes, cheating in the exchange of prisoners of war, exciting slaves to the murder of their masters, plundering private property without a semblance of scruple, burning dwellings, breaking up and destroying agricultural implements, violating female honour, and murdering prisoners in cold blood, not to speak of Greek fire, stone fleets, and other similar expedients of warfare, would scarcely refrain from such trifles as those which excite your indignation. I entertain no doubt whatever that hundreds of thousands of people at the North would be frantic with fiendish delight if informed of the universal massacre of the Southern people, including women and children, in one night. They would then only have to exterminate the blacks (which they are fast doing now), and they would become owners of the property which they covet and for which they are fighting."

About a week before this letter was written Slidell was himself made the object of a little hostile demonstration in Paris.

The day preceding the close of the year Eustis opened the following missive addressed to his chief:

"Paris, December 30, 1863

"His Excellency
Hon. John Slidell

"I write this letter to put you on your guard against a plot on the part of a number of American students (Yankees) at the Lycée Condorcet to make a personal demonstration against you on New Year's Day. Knowing that you habitually leave your residence in the Avenue d'Antin every afternoon for the purpose of visiting your office they purpose waylaying you and subjecting you to indignity. They intend carrying a banner (which I myself have seen) inscribed 'Down with Slidell, the Slave-driver' with an insulting caricature of yourself dragging a slave in chains. They have also composed a song of a most vituperative character which they intend to sing. I do not think they intend any personal assault (they are too cowardly for that!) but it is as well that you should not be taken by surprise.

"I am, Sir,
"With great respect,
"Your sincere well-wisher.
"L. D.
"A Student at the Lycée."

Eustis counselled advising the police, but the Commissioner would not hear of it.

"Let these young Yankee fire-brands have their prank," he said. "An assault on an old gentleman of seventy will redound greatly to their credit. And then, remember it may be only a *canard.*"

On New Year's Day both Eustis and Vignaud had departed to pay calls, when Slidell set out for his usual afternoon stroll. He visited his office and was returning about four o'clock, when he noticed a group of about twenty young men and boys at the corner of the Champs-Elysées. At sight of him they instantly began cat-calling and booing; he proceeded calmly on his walk; they followed in his wake at a safe distance singing "Hang Jeff Davis to a sour-apple-tree" and other choice Union ballads. They carried a crude banner such as that described by his informant. A few were armed with pea-shooters, whose missiles fell harmlessly about the venerable statesman, although one or two found their mark. On the opposite side of the avenue, however, one or two of the youngsters grew bolder and approaching closely aimed wads of paper straight at his face. This was too much for Slidell, who by a rapid flank movement turned upon one youth, seized him by the collar and soundly cuffed him. His companions showed their mettle by taking to their heels. The youngster struggling, as became his principles, for freedom, relinquished his overcoat which remained in Slidell's hands. Two gendarmes appearing, the valiant procession's banner and all utterly vanished from the scene.

On arriving home the representative of the Confederacy exhibited the garment to his family. "Behold a trophy, my dears, of my second actual brush with the enemy. The first, with young Fairfax's marines on the *Trent* was a momentary defeat:—this I may claim as a decisive victory."

Next day, the coat, which bore the name of its owner in the lining—a youth of fifteen named Truro, hailing from New York, was sent back to the *Lycée* with Mr. Slidell's compliments.*

Reading the foregoing account of the affair it is amusing to compare it with the version which the United States Consul-General thought it worth while to forward to Secretary Seward:

"Slidell had a fracas yesterday with some Yankee boys on the Champs-Elysées, which is in all mouths this morning. They had been out sailing their boats in the Bois de Boulogne. Coming back, they met him and made the Union flags on their boats as conspicuous as possible when he passed. Afterwards one of them fired a popgun, which struck him in the back —the boy says by accident. Slidell turned, collared

* Eustis Papers.

the boy, and raised his umbrella to strike him. The boy followed the example of Joseph in the hands of Potiphar's wife and left nothing but his coat in the arms of the Commissioner, who bore it off, not knowing what else to do with it, while the boy left him to his embarrassment. The boy's name is Trouro, I believe, from New Orleans."

CHAPTER VI

BRAVAY & CO.

WHILE the lengthy drama of illicit shipbuilding was unfolding itself in France, Captain Bulloch had been engaged in another in England even more exciting, in which the four Laird rams were concerned.

Let us turn back to the beginning of the story.

From an early date in the war the Confederate naval authorities had determined to build several ironclad vessels of a certain type abroad for operations on the Southern coast. . . . To build them in the South was impracticable: they had neither materials nor mechanics. Had they possessed both, there was no mill in the country to roll the plates, furnaces or machinery to forge them or shops to build the engines. Secretary Mallory in January, 1862, had written that Bulloch ought to have no trouble getting them built in England because "the evident change of feeling and opin-

ion in England in relation to our country induces me
to believe that we may now contract for their construction and delivery."

But Bulloch was shortly to discover the vanity of
such optimism. He was given no end of trouble and
difficulty over the *Alabama* and the *Florida*. The shipyards where they were being constructed swarmed
with Northern spies, and the United States Minister,
Adams, was fulminating daily against the alleged
complicity of the British Government. He felt convinced that such an enterprise was in the highest degree risky and that the Foreign Enlistment Act would
be most rigorously enforced in respect to all undertak-
ings on behalf of the Confederate Government.

"I offered them, therefore," Bulloch related subsequently, "a far safer plan. I suggested that wooden vessels be laid down at once at the various ports of the
South, where timber is abundant, and then send over
scale drawings or working plans of their decks and
sides. After that the iron plates, rivets, bolts, and so
forth, could be made abroad, marked and shipped so
as to arrive on the completion of the hulls."

But it appeared that Jefferson Davis and the Cabinet
were impressed by the belief that Seward's arrogant
despatches and the excessive harshness with which the
right of search and capture was inflicted on neutral

shipping would so irritate the maritime powers that they would not be over-strict in pressing their neutrality laws. So a million dollars was sent over to Bulloch with instructions to get the two ironclads built in England. Bulloch went to Laird Brothers, who had built the *Alabama,* and they agreed to deliver the first of the ships as specified in March, 1863, and the second in May following. The cost of each, fully equipped, but without magazines and battery, was to be £93,750. The Lairds treated with him as a private individual and the contract was a purely "commercial" transaction. In order to avoid any possible appearance of an intent to arm them within British jurisdiction, no magazines were to be placed in either ship, nor any special places for stowing shells and ordnance stores. Nevertheless, the Messrs. Laird took counsel's opinion at the outset as to whether armour-plating a vessel could be construed as "equipment" within the meaning of the Foreign Enlistments Act and were assured that there was nothing illegal in the proposed transaction. Six months later (Sept. 10, 1862), Bulloch reported:

> "The work is going on to my entire satisfaction and if funds do not fail, you shall have two formidable ships ready in the early spring.... At the proper time I will suggest the means of getting officers out

for these ships. For the present I think they had better not be sent here. The presence of a number of
naval officers in England could not fail to excite
comment, and their movements would be closely
watched."

He added that he was already embarrassed by the
number of so-called Confederate agents who turned
up in London and Liverpool, men who were indiscreet and given to promiscuous gossip.

Time wore on and delays occurred in construction.
The Captain grew anxious. The object of the armoured
ships was too evident for further effective disguise.
Even if he succeeded in getting them out of port
on completion, how were they to be officered and
manned? His own idea was to send them out to a
rendezvous at Madeira; but this presented obstacles.
Now another notion occurred to the authorities at
Richmond.

"Go over at once to Paris and see Mr. Slidell and
learn from him whether you cannot fit out the vessels
at a French port, in which event the officers could go
to France, *incognito,* via England, in the ordinary way
and escape observation."

Bulloch acted on these instructions. He told Slidell
that the long-feared danger that the British Government would prevent the departure of the two Birken-

head ironclads was imminent; prompt action was necessary. The vessels must be transferred to some French citizen, removed from England and fitted out in France. How could this best be done?

"I will consult with M. Arman," said Slidell. "Perhaps he will show us a way out of the difficulty."

Arman happened to be attending the opera that evening with his family; but no time need be lost on that account. Eustis was sent out to purchase a couple of stalls for *Don Giovanni*. At the end of the first act Slidell sent a message to Arman, who promptly joined the Confederate Commissioner and his naval friend and colleague. While walking up and down the foyer, the whole matter was discussed and Arman said, "I think I know the very man you want."

He then told them about a certain M. Bravay, who with his brother traded as Bravay & Co., Egyptian and Oriental commission merchants in the rue de Londres.

On the following afternoon, Arman visited Slidell's office, accompanied by a dark-skinned, portly gentleman of about forty, of a decidedly Hebraic cast of features. It was the younger Bravay who had, it appeared, passed some years in Egypt where he had engaged in various operations, some of them on behalf of the Viceroy of that country. His connection with

the Viceroy was known, for there were a dozen tradesmen in Paris, from Worth the couturier to Menier,
the chocolate-maker, whose goods had passed through
Messrs. Bravay's hands en route to palaces on the Nile
and adjacent vice-regal harems. Why, therefore, should
His Highness not order a yacht—a couple of yachts,
an ironclad even, which might be a gift to his Majesty
the Sultan, suzerain lord of Egypt? Such a story could
be made very plausible.

Bravay entered with enthusiasm into the plot. His
firm in Paris would take possession of the two Confederate ironclads, which had been provisionally named
the 290 and the 291, alleging that they had been ordered on behalf of their client, the Pasha of Egypt.
Such an exchange of property required to be managed
with great circumspection. The true ownership of the
vessels was a *secret de polchinelle,* and any attempt to
equip them for sea or even to launch them would result in their seizure and indefinite detention. They
were being watched day and night—Minister Adams
in London was ever on the alert. There was sure to be
a legal enquiry into the title to the property and all
papers and letters relating to the sale must be capable
of bearing the closest official scrutiny and seemingly
prove the *bona fide* character of the pretended sale.
Laird, the builder, would naturally be the principal

witness and it was therefore necessary to pull the wool adroitly over his eyes, and so prevent him from suspecting any collusion between Bulloch and the Bravays. The first step therefore was to concoct a formal letter from Bulloch to the Birkenhead firm. The letter stated that the interference of the British Government in all attempts to build ships suspected of being for the Confederate service was such as to make it certain that Messrs. Laird would not be allowed to complete the ironclads for Bulloch; that the latter was not willing to run the risk of their seizure and the loss of his money; and he requested them to sell the ships for such sum as would ensure a reasonable profit and release him from all further obligations under the contract.

The next step was for Messrs. Bravay to write to Laird applying for tenders for the construction of two ships in the ordinary way of business, as the firm had an illustrious client in Egypt who required them. M. François Bravay had actually been in Egypt in the previous December, so a letter was forthwith composed and antedated "Alexandria, 28th December, 1862," and addressed to his brother Adrien in Paris. We do not know which of the conspirators most enjoyed drafting the various epistles which formed the Bravay *dossier:* but the following was done by Eustis.

"MY DEAR BROTHER:

"I write you a few lines to inform you that the Viceroy positively wishes me to complete some commissions for him, in spite of the reluctance I have manifested to him not to execute them. He has ordered me to have built for him in France two armoured frigates, after the best and most perfect designs. He stipulates above everything that it shall not be made known that they are for the Egyptian Government, for he has political reasons for that.

"Make arrangements to get designs and the contracts in the best form."

To this ingenious missive of course a reply must be forthcoming. It should preferably be from the firm, and somewhat more formal. Thus:

"Your letter of December 28th last transmits to us the commission which his Highness, the Viceroy, has given to have built in France two armoured frigates, after the latest models.

"We will at once take the necessary steps for the execution of that order, in obtaining from the French Government the same facilities for its execution that have been already granted us in reference to the cannon we have had cast for his Highness."

"But why *in France?*" enquired Bravay, on reading the draft. Bulloch explained that this would at once make the Lairds more eager to get the order, besides putting them off the scent.

The foregoing letters with their disarming verisimilitude were approved. Many others were necessary, in order to illustrate the relations of Bravay & Co. and especially M. François Bravay with the opulent and extravagant Pasha. Eustis being credited with a talent for fiction, he was constantly in request. On one occasion, knowing little about Egypt, he had to send out to Galignani's lending library for a few choice works on the Pashalate, in order to provide local colour. As Captain Bulloch pointed out:

"We must have the status of Bravay & Co. fully established, because the Lairds will not pay attention to an offer coming from irresponsible parties." A further convincing touch was given to the *dossier* by a number of genuine letters from the firm's agent in Egypt.

When all seemed in order and the letters despatched, it was thought prudent for Bulloch to remain in Paris and set about the task of procuring crews for the vessels when released. It would be embarrassing for him to be seen anywhere in the vicinity of Birkenhead.

What happened next was disconcerting. After the Messrs. Laird got Bulloch's letter desiring them to find a purchaser for the rams, they learned that the Russian Government actually sought just such a pair of vessels and would be happy to purchase them! Bravay's letter containing a definite demand for a tender followed. The Lairds would have preferred Russia, and an order to build new ships, but Bravay's representation of the Viceroy's impatience, reinforced by Bravay's personal visit to their yard and entire satisfaction with the vessels carried the day. The Egyptian Pasha should not be disappointed.

Ensued a period of hope, but of hope perpetually deferred. August came and the rams remained unfinished in dock, while Federal suspicions grew stronger and their spies bolder. British officials, egged on by Adams, became insufferable, besetting the Lairds with awkward enquiries as to the real ownership and destination of the unlucky rams. At last the builders, in order to relieve the situation, insisted that Bravay & Co. should avow their ownership, which they accordingly did. A few days later a British naval officer, Captain Hore, R. N., appeared in Paris and paid a visit to Bravay & Co. in the rue de Londres. Her Majesty's Government, he said, had instructed him to make enquiries as to the object of the firm in acquiring two such formidable ships. To all his questions Messrs. Bravay made satisfactory answers and frankly exhibited the correspondence. At the close of this interview Captain Hore made a direct offer to purchase the ships for the British Admiralty, a proposal which the Frenchmen declined to entertain, at least, they added, until the vessels had been completed according to the designs and were delivered at a French port. The naval officer then retired and Adrien Bravay jumped into a fiacre and drove to the rue Marignan to relate to Slidell all that had happened.

As for Bulloch he feared the worst. He knew that at this crucial moment he ought to keep away from Liverpool, yet he was obliged to be there occasionally, especially to receive and send reports by the Bermuda mail, and to interview officers. He was advised to adopt a disguise, but although he shaved off his beard and assumed an outlandish dress, yet every time he found shrewd Yankee eyes fastened upon him. They even swore to his constant presence, superintending the implicated ships, which he angrily denied; he was there only for a day or two a month. Bulloch, reviewing events later, wrote:

> "Matters continued to grow worse at Liverpool. The nature of some of the affidavits sent up to the Foreign Office by the United States Consul leaked out and although some of them were glaringly false, still they seemed to be whispered into willing ears

and had such an effect that the Lairds were directed not to attempt a trial trip with either ship without giving notice to the Customs officials; and were finally forbidden to do so at all, except with a squad of Marines or other force from one of her Majesty's ships on board." *

Finally, on October 9th, the two rams were virtually seized by the British Government, on the ground that a number of Confederate naval officers who had just come from France were plotting to capture them and forcibly take them out of Liverpool.

"But could this be done?" Slidell enquired, when Bulloch reported this.

"Impossible," Bulloch explained. "One of the rams is in the Great Birkenhead Float, as it is called. To be got out she must pass through a kind of lock; a large caisson must be lifted, which can only be done at a certain stage of the tide; and finally, a gate requiring machinery to move it must be opened to give her egress. If it were desired to move her from the dock, the keeper would require five hours' notice. Yet the British Government have thought it necessary to place a gunboat with extra marines alongside of her, the fasts of the gunboat being actually placed over those of the ram, and for days have kept a sixty-gun frigate

* Bulloch to Mallory, October 20th, 1863.

at anchor opposite the dock-gate, for fear this formidable ship might jump over all these obstructions and go to sea in charge of our officers and discharged seamen who have been waiting in the offing, without bending a sail or lighting a fire."

Bulloch spoke bitterly. As to the other ram, being in a less advanced state, she was consequently less under surveillance.

Slidell then told Bulloch of what had come to his knowledge, of a body of desperate men, several of them Frenchmen, who had left France for Liverpool with, he feared, the intention of somehow getting possession of one of the rams and with the aid of some of the dockyard men getting her out of the dock and out to sea.

"It is pure madness," said Bulloch, "and I shall discountenance any such scheme."

Yet he knew that Captain Barron and the young officers surrounding him were desperate, that their long inaction in Paris had grown intolerable. Day after day they had called at the Commissioner's office for news, they had haunted the Naval Agent's house at Auteuil, nightly they had met at the Grand Hotel and devised wild plans to put an end to their idleness, even to taking service under France in Mexico or fitting out an English yacht for a privateering foray.

"We must have those ships," declared Bulloch, "but there is only one way we can get hold of them now. They are the property of a French subject and the French Government must come forward and claim them. Bravay should have avowed their ownership from the first instead of allowing it to leak out, and have asked permission to complete them. If the answer had been 'No' then we could have sold the ships in reality and put the money to other pressing uses."

Slidell counselled patience. He said he was negotiating with the Emperor himself, that Bulloch should not interfere or dictate too much to Messrs. Bravay in the management of details; and that in spite of the seizure, he was in hopes of inducing the French Government to intervene and demand the restitution of the ships.

Meantime, there was much to engage the energy of both Slidell and Bulloch in the ships which Arman was building for them at Bordeaux and by the dramatic arrival of the *Florida* at Brest and of her captain Maffitt in Paris.

Not until the 2nd of February, 1864, did the hopes of Slidell and Bulloch as regards Imperial intervention finally fall to the ground. Napoleon caused the Messrs. Bravay and the other parties concerned to be informed that he could not make a request to the British Government to release the rams. This was

hardly surprising considering that the Federal suspicions attaching to the transaction with Bravay had
been confirmed. On October 19, 1863, Thayer, the
United States Consul-General in Egypt, had written
to Nubar Pasha the following note:

> "My dear Sir,
> "I am informed that the Viceroy has entered into
> or is negotiating a contract for the construction of
> one or more vessels of war to be built in France. If
> the request is a proper one, will you kindly inform
> me if this report is correct and in that case who is to
> have the contract when the vessel or vessels are to be
> built. I need hardly say to you that my motive in ad-
> dressing these questions to you is not to gratify an
> idle curiosity."

But this was a little crude and the inquisitive American was informed that Nubar Pasha had no information concerning his Highness's intentions to furnish
him. So a Federal agent was sent to Egypt and the
question put direct to the Viceroy, who denied any
knowledge of the alleged transaction. At last, then,
the fat was in the fire.

Bulloch was formally advised that there was no
longer any hope of getting the ships out and there
was nothing left for him to do but to recover, if he
could, the money expended. A law action was

promptly begun in the English courts and the elder
Bravay went to Egypt to see if he could induce the
Viceroy to change his attitude.

After the formal seizure on October 9th the two
ships were kept literally in a state of siege at Birkenhead.

> "The Government," reported Bullock, "had been
> persuaded by Mr. Adams that the discharged crew
> of the *Florida* had been sent to Liverpool for the pur-
> pose of forcibly seizing the rams and taking them
> out to sea, and if there had been a hostile fleet off the
> harbour, Captain Inglefield could not have been
> more perplexed and anxious, more nervously active
> and watchful in his precautions and preparations to
> discover and defeat a cutting-out expedition than he
> appears to have been with respect to the alleged hos-
> tile seamen from the *Florida,* who were probably
> smoking their pipes at the Sailor's Home or were al-
> ready dispersed in other ships, in happy or careless
> unconsciousness of the agitation they were creating."

Not until May, 1864, after a great deal of legal
pother in which both the Lairds and the Bravays were
threatened with forfeiture, did the British Government name a price for the rams. This was accepted
and the two vessels passed into the Royal Navy. As a
commercial transaction the Confederate Government
had no reason to complain, as the price was some

£30,000 in excess of what they had spent and the cash thus realised came at a moment when it was sadly needed.

When the news reached Richmond the "hopes shared by thousands were prostrated," and the "bitterness of disappointment" was felt over "this great national misfortune." For it is hardly too much to say that these two ships might have changed entirely the fortunes of the Confederacy. As Bulloch had written enthusiastically from Paris in July, 1863:

> "After getting their crews on board off Wilmington, our vessels might sail southward, sweep the blockading fleet from the sea-front of every harbour from the Capes of Virginia to Sabine Pass and cruising up and down the coast, could prevent anything like permanent systematic interruption of our foreign trade for the future. Again, should Washington still be held by the enemy, our ironclads should ascend the Potomac, and after destroying all transports and gunboats falling within their reach, could render Washington itself untenable and could thus create a powerful diversion in favour of any operations General Lee might have on foot."

Portsmouth, New Hampshire, was a wealthy town which would lie at their mercy.

> "Suppose our two ironclads should steam unannounced into that harbour some fine October

morning and while one proceeded to demolish the navy yard and all it contained, the other should send a flag of truce to the mayor, to say that if $1,000,000 in gold or $5,000,000 in greenbacks were not sent on board in four hours the city would be destroyed.... Philadelphia is another point open to such an attack. Once in front of the city they could dictate their own terms."

It was a delightful picture, and Slidell could not fail to share its author's enthusiasm. One aged Confederate veteran recalls that Bulloch kept a copy of that joyous letter always in his pocket "to revive the drooping spirits of some of his young officers whenever they saw their chances of ever embarking on a glorious raid receding gradually into the limbo of unfought battles and the melancholy realm of the might-have-been." *

But when the disappointment of all parties is considered, it is yet probable that the two most disgusted men in France in connection with the affair, were the two brothers Bravay and in particular M. Adrien. They had got their commission, it is true, but they had been utterly discredited in at least four capitals. Mr. Charles Francis Adams had publicly pilloried Adrien as "a French commercial adventurer,

* Letter of J. S. Rhead.

proved to have been capable of prevarication, if not of absolute falsehood," while the Viceroy of Egypt referred to him as "a scheming French rascal who nearly succeeded in getting me into a mess with the Sultan."

Perhaps, therefore, it is hardly surprising that one day when they were passing along the Boulevard des Italiens, Mr. Slidell and M. Bravay mutually failed to recognise one another and passed on with faces utterly blank. Moreover, even so zealous and staunch a French supporter as M. Arman was beginning to feel nervous about the issue of his maritime intrigues on behalf of the Southern Confederacy.

CHAPTER VII

CERTAIN ZEALOUS INTERMEDIARIES

IT is probable that there was no keener protago-
nist of the Confederacy or a more pugnacious member of the British House of Commons than John
Arthur Roebuck, M.P. for Sheffield. Brought up in
Canada he had there imbibed (as he himself avowed)
"a cordial detestation of the Yankees." He had already
shown himself on two notable occasions in 1837 and
in 1855 a dreaded Opposition firebrand. Carlyle once
met him at a Radical dinner party and wrote:

"Roebuck Robespierre was there, an acrid, barren,
sandy character, dissonant-speaking dogmatist, trivial
with a singular exasperation; restlessness as of diseased
vanity written all over his face when you come near it.
I do not think him equal to Robespierre."

This is a jaundiced picture, for Roebuck was a man
of parts and eloquence, as well as incorruptible. He
had zealously taken up the cause of the South and in

June, 1863, announced that he was going to move a resolution in favour of recognition by the British Government. With him was associated a prominent fellow-member, a Liverpool shipmaster, J. A. Lindsay, who had written many letters and pamphlets in favour of the Confederacy. His intention to move such a resolution was much advertised and was fixed for June 30, two or three weeks ahead. Naturally, much importance was attached in the Confederate camp to this motion, as forcing the hand of the Government.

One evening Roebuck had a conversation with a former Under Secretary of State and he wrote thus to Lindsay:

> "Seymour Fitzgerald said to me last night that it was rumoured that the French Emperor at the present time thought it would be unwise to recognise the South and that Lord Palmerston on the 30th would say that England thought the time for recognition had not arrived; that France, he could state authoritatively, thought so, too, and that therefore it was quite clear that any negotiations about the matter at the present time were utterly out of place and impossible. Now, upon this an idea has come into my head, and I will explain it by a question. Could we, that is, you and I, do any good by going to Paris and seeing the Emperor?

"You know that I am no great admirer of that great Personage; but still I am a politician—so is he —and politicians have no personal likes or dislikes that stand in the way of their political ends. I therefore would act as if I had no feelings either friendly or hostile to him—he would do the same as regards myself, and therefore I have no fear but that he would listen to all that I have to offer by way of suggestion or advice."

Napoleon was a realist: and this manly outspokenness would probably not have offended him, although Slidell told Benjamin he had omitted the final passage when, as we shall presently see, he read the letter to the Emperor.

The day was June 18, 1863, the anniversary of Waterloo. Slidell had the previous day received from the First Chamberlain, the Duke de Bassano, a note appointing ten o'clock at the Tuileries for the interview with the Emperor. He was again cordially received.

Napoleon said he had read the memorandum of Persigny and was more fully convinced than ever of the propriety of a general recognition by the European Powers of the Confederacy; but the success of his Mexican expedition would be jeopardised by any rupture with the United States. No other Power than

England possessed a sufficient navy to give him efficient aid in a war on the ocean, which, however,
would be obviated if England co-operated.

"Sir," replied Slidell, "I am satisfied that recognition by France and any other Continental Powers, or
even by France alone, will not lead to a war with the
United States. They already find ample occupation for
all their energies at home. We can count on the support of Spain, Austria, Prussia, Belgium, Holland,
Sweden and Denmark."

"None of these Powers," Napoleon reminded him,
"owns a navy of any consequence."

His interlocutor suggested that Spain had a respectable fleet and was constantly increasing it. He was
authorised to pledge the Confederate Government to
a tripartite treaty solemnly guaranteeing the permanent possession of Cuba to Spain, which would, he
thought, induce Spain, if assured of French support,
to take the first step towards recognition. (If the
memory of Slidell's scheming during many years in
Congress to get American possession of Cuba on any
terms occurred to Napoleon at this moment it may
have occasioned an inward smile!)

Would your Majesty, pursued Slidell, give such an
assurance to Spain? Napoleon said he would. Slidell
then asked, "Will your Majesty authorise me to say so

to the Spanish Ambassador, Señor Isturitz, to whom I have already spoken about the Treaty?"

The Emperor replied that he was willing that this should be done.

The moment was now ripe for Slidell to produce Roebuck's letter to his friend and colleague, Lindsay. He took it from his pocket and read it to the Emperor, dwelling with emphasis on the passage relating to the Emperor's alleged intentions.

"May I ask your Majesty **if such a rumour is correct?"**

"You may give it an unqualified denial," promptly answered Napoleon.

Slidell then said that Roebuck and his friend Lindsay were most anxious to have a talk with his Majesty about the former's forthcoming motion in Parliament. Would it be agreeable to him to receive these staunch friends of the Confederacy? The Emperor replied that he would be happy to see them.

After a pause he added: "I think that I can do something better: I will make a direct proposition to England for joint recognition. This will effectually prevent Lord Palmerston from misrepresenting my position and wishes on the American question. I shall bring the question before the Cabinet Meeting to-day, and if it should be decided not to make the proposition now, I will let you know in a day or two through M. Mocquard what to say to Mr. Roebuck."

Having thus disposed of the chief business of his visit Slidell felt that he could now indulge in conversational by-paths:

"'It may perhaps be an indiscretion to ask whether your Majesty prefers to see the Whigs or Tories in power in England.' Napoleon answered, 'I rather prefer the Whigs.' I remarked that Lord Malmesbury would under a Conservative administration probably be the Secretary for Foreign Affairs, and that I had always understood that intimate relations existed between the Emperor and him. He said, 'That is true; personally we are excellent friends, but personal relations have very little influence in great affairs where party interests are involved.' He playfully remarked, 'The Tories are very good friends of mine when in a minority, but their tone changes very much when they get into power.'

"He then spoke of the different spirit with which the news of the fall of Puebla * had been received North and South; that the Northern papers showed their disappointment and hostility, while Richmond had been illuminated on the occasion. This is reported by the newspapers. I, of course, did not express any doubt of the fact, although I considered it some-

* Captured by a French force Feb. 17, 1863.

what apocryphal. I said there could be no doubt of
the bitterness of the Northern people at the success of
his arms in Mexico, while all our sympathies were
with France, and urged the importance of securing
the lasting gratitude and attachment of a people already so well disposed; that there could be no doubt
that our Confederacy was to be the strongest power
of the American Continent, and that our alliance was
worth cultivating. He said that he was quite convinced of the fact and spoke with great admiration
of the bravery of our troops, the skill of our generals
and the devotion of our people. He expressed his
great regret at the death of Stonewall Jackson, whom
he considered one of the most remarkable men of
the age.

"I expressed my thanks to him for his sanction of
the contract made for the building of four ships of
war at Bordeaux and Nantes. I then informed him
that we were prepared to build several ironclad ships
of war and that I only required his verbal assurance
that they should be allowed to proceed to sea under
the Confederate flag to enter into contracts for these.
He said we might build the ships but it would be
necessary that their destination should be concealed.
... The permission to build, equip and proceed to sea
would be no violation of neutrality. I invoked the
precedent of a ship built for the Chilean government
under the circumstances mentioned in my despatch of
20th April. The Emperor remarked that there was

a distinction to be drawn between that case and what I desired to do. Chile was a government recognised by France."

Roebuck and Lindsay duly notified M. Mocquard of their arrival in Paris and received a request to come to Fontainebleau. There they had their promised interview with the Emperor. As Roebuck afterwards wrote to Slidell:

"His Majesty told me that he, on hearing that a rumour was prevalent in London that he had changed his mind on the subject of recognition, had sent instructions to Baron Gros to deny the truth of that rumour, and, further, that he had instructed his Ambassador to enquire of the English Government whether they were prepared now to entertain the question of recognition, and to state that if they were so, he, the Emperor, was ready to act with them and would be glad of their resolution.

"I suggested to his Majesty that he, through his Ambassador, should make a formal proposal to that effect to the English Government; his Majesty thereupon said to me that he could not do so, and would tell me the reason why. Some time last year he had made such a formal proposition to England; and his despatch had been sent to Lord Lyons, by whom it had been shown to Mr. Seward, who had complained to the French Minister at Washington of these his Majesty's proceedings. 'Now,' said the Emperor, 'I deem myself ill-treated in this matter, and I cannot subject myself again to be so dealt with.'"

With this Roebuck and Lindsay had to be content and they returned to London. On the 30th, before a crowded House of Commons, Roebuck arose and presented his motion to request the British Government to negotiate with the European Powers with a view to recognising the Confederate States of America. In order to show, as he subsequently explained, "that this proposal was a wise one," he stated that the French Emperor had personally given him permission to tell the House exactly what had passed at the Fontainebleau interview. This he proceeded to do.

Roebuck's statement created a sensation. During the ensuing debate it was divulged that the French Ambassador had gone straight to Earl Russell and denied ever having received any instructions of such a character from the Emperor. Sir George Grey told the House that "nothing of the sort described by Mr. Roebuck with reference to the Emperor's despatch had occurred." After this, the opinion of the members was that "either Roebuck or Napoleon III was lying."

Matters could not rest thus; so Roebuck wrote instantly to Slidell that Grey " 'did not in the least doubt my veracity,' thereby plainly insinuating that the want of truth was on the other side of the Channel.

> "Now, I am anxious that his Majesty should know on my authority that such things were said last night. His Majesty will know full well that I told simply what he said to me, and he will be able to ascertain where the error lies. I cannot presume to write myself to his Majesty; but it has suggested itself to me that you by some means can have this letter laid before his Majesty. The debate will be resumed in a week; I have the right of reply and should be greatly delighted if his Majesty would kindly give me the means of making the requisite explanations."

Feeling that he was embarked on a very delicate business Slidell forwarded Roebuck's request to Mocquard, with whom he was on intimate terms, and some days later received the following:

> "Fontainebleau, July 6, 1863
> "My dear Mr. Slidell:
> "You will find enclosed a note I am requested to send you in reply to the letter of which you desired me to make the communication. Please to receive, my dear Mr. Slidell, the renewed assurance of my best and affectionate feelings.
> "Mocquard."

The note which accompanied this had been dictated by Napoleon.

"The Emperor having been informed fifteen days ago that the report had been spread to London of H. M. having changed his opinion as regards the recognition of the South, M. Drouyn de Lhuys wrote to Baron Gros that he should refute the said report.

"Meantime Messrs. Roebuck and Lindsay came over and paid a visit to the Emperor, whom they invited to make an official application to the British Cabinet towards the recognition of the South. H. M. replied that such a step was not practicable before knowing whether it would be agreed to; since the first proposal of mediation had met with a denial, and H. M. had been told (a thing of which he had, in truth, no proof) that the cabinet of London boasted at Washington of declining such of the Emperor's proposals as were in favour of the South. Now, H. M. has neither cause nor feeling of animosity toward the United States, and it is but with the hope of seeing an end put to a war already too long that he considered the recognition of the South as a speedier means to bring about peace. The Emperor could not have spoken to Mr. Roebuck of any despatch or despatches exhibited by Lord Lyons to Mr. Seward, because there was none but those which have been published.

> "However, his Majesty regrets Mr. Roebuck's mak-
> ing public an entirely confidential explanation." *

After this explanation and rebuke, Roebuck's
motion ended in utter failure and the lengthy speech
which his friend Lindsay had composed in its support
was never delivered.

Recognition of the South could easily command a
majority in Parliament; but recognition of the South
which implied an approbation of slavery was not practical politics.

In September, 1863, the Slidells followed the Court
to Biarritz, from whence Slidell wrote (September
16):

> "My family and I have been twice to the receptions
> of the Empress. She received Mrs. S. and the girls
> most graciously. At these parties men are not pre-
> sented to her but at her request. On both occasions
> she sent for me, on the first she talked with me for
> more than twenty minutes. She is perfectly well
> posted about our affairs, and understands the ques-
> tion in all its bearings thoroughly. At my second
> visit she conversed probably ten or twenty minutes

* On the day following the interview of Roebuck and Lindsay
with the Emperor, Drouyn de Lhuys did telegraph to Baron Gros
to inform Lord Palmerston "officiously" that should Great Britain
be willing to recognise the South the Emperor would be ready to
follow suit.

and was very particular in enquiring about the siege of Charleston.

"She sympathises most warmly with our cause and so expresses herself without any reserve. I mention these facts because the Empress is supposed, I believe with truth, to exercise considerable influence in public affairs.

"...I forgot to mention that the Emperor at the second reception of the Empress was present—he came to me and shook hands and conversed very cordially for several minutes."

William Lowndes Yancey, whom forty years later Woodrow Wilson came to eulogise as the "fiery soul" of the Secessionist cause, had returned home to die, and his successor, Mason, under the constant lash of Minister Adams had temporarily retired into the English countryside. It was then that the third member of the original Confederate triumvirate in Europe, the redoubtable Colonel Dudley Mann, came to Paris and unfolded to Slidell a new and ambitious project.

This same Dudley Mann had led a chequered career. There was a British Consul at Charleston, South Carolina, named Bunch, who early in the war thus reported to the Foreign Office:

"His appointment [as European Commissioner with Yancey] has given great dissatisfaction to many persons in the South, partly on account of his personal

character, which is not good. He is the son of a bank-
rupt grocer and is credited with some knowledge of
'Court life' on account of his having got himself on
various European missions, one of which as far back
as 1850 was to encourage the Hungarians in their
struggle with Austria. For this the Austrian Minister
in Washington informed the Secretary of State that
his Government 'would hang Mr. Mann without
scruple.' He was," concluded Consul Bunch, "a 'trading politician' and interested in an attempt to establish a direct steamship line from New Orleans and
Charleston to Europe. He is a personal friend of Jefferson Davis, but has no special merit of any description."

This is perhaps rather too sweeping: and passes over
some of Mann's merits, amongst which were an
exuberance of credulous enthusiasm and an imposing
physical presence.

Emperors and Kings had failed the Southern cause
and trust had vainly been put in the Princes of the
Earth. There was one ruler to whom as yet no appeal
had been made and he the most august of all. If the
Supreme Pontiff of Christendom, Pius X, were to
espouse their cause, the effect upon world opinion
would be incalculable.

"I propose," wrote Mann to Slidell, "to draw up a

letter to the Pope, to be signed by the President. This I myself, in the capacity of special envoy to his Holiness, will carry to Rome. I have exposed the plan to Mason, who is, however, disinclined to attach that importance to any expression of papal opinion which millions of believers do." *

Considering the precarious situation which the Pope then occupied in Rome, it may have been thought that his universal prestige had somewhat suffered. But Mann was enthusiastic over his idea. If the Pope received him at all, if he deigned to return any answer to the President's letter, it was tantamount to a recognition of the Confederacy, and tens of thousands of Irish and German troops in the Union armies would forthwith be smitten with religious scruples.

When the Colonel came to Paris to discuss his plan, Slidell could not help expressing a mild surprise that his friend should have been led so late in life into the Romish fold.

Mann smilingly replied:

"I am no more a Roman Catholic than you or than Judah P. Benjamin is. In fact, I do not subscribe to any religious denomination; but I don't underrate the Pope's influence—as universal as it is benign."

He then read a draft of the letter which he had re-

* Eustis Papers.

quested Benjamin to submit to President Davis, beginning "Most Holy Father: May it please your Holiness—"

Three months passed. At the beginning of November, 1863, Mann returned triumphantly to Paris en route to Rome. He was accompanied by his son. The President's letter to the Pope, concocted by an agnostic, revised by a Jew and signed by a Presbyterian, was in his pocket. It was read aloud in its perfected state to Mrs. Slidell and the Commissioner's family, including Father Lebrun, a New Orleans priest, and all enthusiastically approved. Mann then expressed his opinion that a knowledge of his sacred mission should be conveyed to her Majesty, the Empress Eugenie, who might facilitate his reception by the Pope. A copy of the letter was accordingly shown a few days later to the Empress by one of the Court chaplains. As a result, the Papal Nuncio in Paris informed the competent official at the Vatican of the impending arrival of the Honourable A. Dudley Mann, special Envoy of the President of the Confederate States to his Holiness the Pope. Mann had temporarily dropped the appellation of "Colonel" as savouring of secular militarism.

Rome was reached in the first week of November and on the 13th word came to Mann that he would be received by the Pope on the following day. What occurred at this interview Mann related in a lengthy letter to Slidell, which was almost identical with those sent to Mason and Benjamin. If ever a spirit of exaltation entered into a human being, filling him with reverence, humility, and the Christian virtues, it now possessed the soul of this transcendental grocer's son as he gazed upon the Supreme Pontiff. It was, in his own language, the "most thrilling moment of his life," "one of the most remarkable conferences that ever a foreign representative had with a potentate of the earth." After a brief reference to his credentials the visitor handed the precious missive to the Pope. The interview was in French.

"Looking for a moment at the address and afterwards at the seal of the letter, his Holiness took his scissors and cut the envelope. Upon opening it he observed: 'I see it is in English—a language which I do not understand.' I remarked: 'If it will be agreeable to your Holiness, my secretary will translate its contents to you.' He replied: 'I shall be pleased if he will do so.' The translation was rendered in a slow, solemn, and emphatic pronunciation. During its progress I did not cease for an instant to carefully survey the features of the Sovereign Pontiff. A sweeter expression of pious affection, of tender benignity, never adorned the face of mortal man. No

picture can adequately represent him when exclusively absorbed in Christian contemplation. Every
sentence of the letter appeared to sensibly affect him.
At the conclusion of each, he would lay his hand
down upon the desk and bow his head approvingly.
When the passage was reached wherein the President states, in such sublime and affecting language,
'We have offered up at the footstool of our Father
who art in Heaven prayers inspired by the same feeling which animates your Holiness,' his deep sunken
orbs, visibly moistened, were upturned towards that
throne upon which ever sits the Prince of Peace, indicating that his heart was pleading for our deliverance from the causeless and merciless war which is
prosecuted against us. The soul of infidelity—if indeed infidelity have a soul—would have melted in
view of so sacred a spectacle."

The emotion occasioned by the translation was succeeded by a silence of some time. At length His Holiness asked whether President Davis was a Catholic.
Mann answered in the negative. "He then asked if I
was one. I assured him that I was not."

Mann's assurance in all emergencies was unfailing.
But perhaps "assurance" on this occasion was hardly
the *mot juste*.

His Holiness now stated, according to Mann, that
"Lincoln and Co." ("his own language") had endeav-

oured to create an impression abroad that they were fighting for the abolition of slavery and that "it might be judicious in us to consent to gradual emancipation."

"I replied that the subject of slavery was one over which the Government of the Confederate States like that of the old United States, had no control whatever; that all ameliorations with regard to the institution must proceed from the States themselves, which were as sovereign in their character, in this regard, as were France, Austria or any other Continental power; that true philanthropy shuddered at the thought of a liberation of the slave in the manner attempted by Lincoln and Co.; that such a procedure would be practically to convert the well-cared-for civilised negro into a semi-barbarian; that such of our slaves as had been captured or decoyed off by our enemy were in an incomparably worse condition than while they were in the service of their masters: that they wished to return to their old homes, the love of which was the strongest of their affections; that if, indeed, African slavery were an evil, there was a Power which in its own good time would doubtless remove that evil in a more gentle manner than that of causing the earth to be deluged with blood for its sudden overthrow."

Pius IX received these remarks "with an approving expression." He told his visitor that he had reason to

be proud of the self-sacrificing devotion of his countrymen, from the beginning, to the cause for which
they were contending.

"The most ample reason," Mann agreed; "and yet
scarcely so much as of my country*women,* whose patriotism, whose sorrows and privations, whose trans-
formation in many instances from luxury to penury,
were unparalleled, and could not be adequately described by any living language. There they had been
from the beginning, there they were still, more
resolute, if possible than ever—emulating in devotion,
earthly though it was in its character, those holy female spirits who were the last at the Cross and the
first at the Sepulchre."

His Holiness received this rhetoric with evident
satisfaction, and then said: "I would like to do anything that can be effectively done, or that even promises good results, to aid in putting an end to this most
terrible war, which is harming the good of all the
earth, if I knew how to proceed."

Mann thought the moment propitious to inform
the Pope that it was

> "not the armies of Northern birth which the South
> was encountering in hostile array, but that it was the
> armies of European creation—occasioned by the
> Irish and Germans, chiefly the former, who were in-

fluenced to emigrate (by circulars from 'Lincoln and Co.' to their numerous agents abroad) ostensibly for the purpose of securing high wages, but in reality to fill up the constantly depleted ranks of our enemy; that those poor unfortunates were tempted by high bounties—amounting to five hundred, six hundred, and seven hundred dollars—to enlist and take up arms against us; that once in the service they were invariably placed in the most exposed points of danger in the battlefield; that, in consequence thereof, an instance had occurred in which an almost entire brigade had been left dead or wounded upon the ground; that but for the foreign recruits the North would most likely have broken down months ago in the absurd attempt to overpower the South."

Pius expressed his "utter astonishment—repeatedly throwing up his hands—at the employment of such means against us, and the cruelty attendant upon such unscrupulous operations."

"But, your Holiness," pursued Mann, " 'Lincoln & Co.' are even more wicked, if possible, in their ways than in decoying innocent Irishmen from their homes to be murdered in cold blood. Their champions—and would your Holiness believe it, unless it were authoritatively communicated to you?—their pulpit champions have boldly asserted this as a sentiment: 'Greek fire for the families and cities of the rebels, and Hell-fire for their chiefs.'"

"His Holiness was startled at this information and immediately observed, 'Certainly no Catholic would reiterate so monstrous a sentiment.' I replied, 'Assuredly not. It finds a place exclusively in the heart of the fiendish vagrant buffoons whose number is legion and who impiously undertake to teach the doctrine of Christ for ulterior sinister purposes.'"

From which it will be gathered that the ci-devant Colonel was master of a florid speech and had borrowed from his friend Yancey some of the latter's happy invective. The Pope was duly impressed. The interview approached an end.

His Holiness observed: "I will write a letter to President Davis and of such a character that it may be published for general perusal."

Mann was overwhelmed with gratitude.

The Pope then remarked, half inquiringly: "You will remain here for several months?"

To this Mann "could not do otherwise than answer in the affirmative." Besides, he was drawing $1000 a month from the Confederate treasury during the period of his mission.

"Turning to my secretary, he asked several kind questions personal to himself, and bestowed upon him a handsome compliment. He then extended his hand, as a signal for the end of the audience, and I retired."

"Thus," concludes Mann's narrative, "terminated one of the most remarkable conferences that ever a foreign representative had with a potentate of the earth. And such a potentate! A potentate who wields the consciences of one hundred and seventy-five millions of the civilised race, and who is adored by that immense number as the Vicegerent of God in this lunary sphere.

"How strikingly majestic the conduct of the Government of the Pontifical States in its bearing towards me when contrasted with the sneaking subterfuges to which some of the Governments of western Europe have had recourse in order to evade intercourse with our commissioners! Here I was openly received at the Department of Foreign Affairs— openly received by an appointment at Court, in accordance with established usages and customs, and treated from beginning to end with a consideration which might be envied by the envoy of the oldest member of the family of nations!"

What a triumph! Where were Lords Russell and Palmerston now? Where was that canting Yankee envoy, Charles Francis Adams?

For a month after his audience Mann waited in Rome for Pope Pius's reply to Jefferson Davis's letter.

He and his son spent their time in the august society
of cardinals and bishops, and in visiting churches. The
atmosphere which he breathed daily could not fail to
have an effect upon his moral nature. He who had
fought three duels (as his son avowed to George
Eustis) lost his former truculence and began to feel
the stirrings of native piety within him. In reply to
Slidell's congratulations on the good impression he
seemed to have made on the Pope, he wrote that he
regarded himself "but as an instrument in the hand of
Providence."

He was to attain greater heights than this. For on
December 9 came Pius IX's answer, and Dudley
Mann was transported with felicity.

Today, reading this epistle calmly and coolly we
find very little in it. It is benevolent, it is brief; it is in
impeccable Latin. It recites that the Pontiff had, in
previous years, addressed letters to the Archbishops of
New York and New Orleans urging them to employ
their earnest efforts "in order that the fatal Civil War
which had arisen in the States should end and that the
people of America might again enjoy mutual peace
and love each other with mutual charity." Addressing
the Confederate President it continues:

"It has been very gratifying to us to recognise,
Illustrious Sir, that you and your people are ani-

mated by the same desire for peace and tranquillity which we had so earnestly inculcated in our
aforesaid letter to the Venerable Brethren above
named. Oh, that the other people also of the States
and their rulers, considering seriously how cruel and
how deplorable is this intestine war, would receive
and embrace the councils of peace and tranquillity!
We indeed shall not cease with fervent prayers to be-
seech God, the best and Highest, and to implore
Him to pour out the spirit of Christian love and
peace upon all the people of America, and to rescue
them from the great calamities with which they are
afflicted. And we also pray the same most merciful
Lord that He will illumine your Excellency with the
light of His divine grace, and unite you with ourselves in perfect charity."

That was all. No Pope, however little he favoured
the Confederate cause, could have done less. But a
papal paraphrase of the Sermon on the Mount was,
one may hazard, hardly what the occasion demanded.
The world has seen, both before and since, papal ency-
clicals breathing denunciation and threatening dire
retribution towards offenders: scorching blasts from
St. Peter's which have actually diverted the actions and
tendencies of nations and their rulers. To this category
the letter of Pius IX to Jefferson Davis manifestly did
not belong. Yet had it been such an epochal utterance

the satisfaction of Colonel Dudley Mann could hardly have been greater.

"We are *acknowledged,*" he exclaims exultantly, in a letter (December 9) "by as high an authority as this world contains, to be an *independent Power of the Earth!*"

Whence this "acknowledgment?" Because the Pope has addressed his letter "to the illustrious and Honourable Jefferson Davis, President of the Confederate States of America," a title which for nearly three years had been withheld by England, France, Russia and the rest. Mann wrote, ecstatically, to Benjamin:

> "I congratulate you. I congratulate the President. I congratulate his Cabinet; in short I congratulate all my true-hearted countrymen and countrywomen, upon this benign event. The hand of the Lord has been in it and eternal glory and praise be to His Holy and Righteous Name.
>
> "The example of the Sovereign Pontiff, if I am not much mistaken, will exercise a salutary influence upon both the Catholic and Protestant Governments of Western Europe. Humanity will be aroused everywhere to the importance of its early emulation."
>
> "The document is in the Latin language," the writer explains, "as are all documents prepared by the Pope. I cannot incur the risk of its capture at sea and therefore I shall retain it until I can convey

it with entire certainty to the President. It will adorn
the archives of our country in all coming time."

He therefore delayed his departure from Rome for
some weeks further while a copy and a translation
were being made.

The question now arose, how were the glad tidings
of the papal recognition of the Confederacy to be
broadcast throughout the universe?

Did Slidell think he should await the actual receipt
of the letter by the President?

But by that time Slidell had come largely to discount Mann's efforts and to attach little importance to
the papal letter. Much more useful, he thought, was
Mann's report of his interview and the Pope's reprehension of the Northern recruiting methods, and this
ought to be widely circulated as a check on Federal
enlistments. Mann passed through Paris on his way to
London, bearing the precious letter which he was
ready to exhibit to all and sundry, "as if," said Eustis,
"it were a fragment of the True Cross."

As to papal recognition, Slidell called on the
Nuncio to ascertain whether it had any diplomatic
value and was informed that that dignitary had received "no instructions to put his official visa on our
passports" as Mann's assertions had led him to
suppose would be forthcoming.

Mann's report and the Pope's letter had, however, been transmitted to the Empress Eugénie and had caused her Majesty "deep satisfaction."

Not until March, 1864, did Dudley Mann receive an acknowledgment from Richmond, not, as he had hoped, from Jefferson Davis himself, but by the secretarial hand of Judah P. Benjamin. The President (he was told)

> "has been much gratified at learning the cordial reception which you received from the Pope.... As a recognition of the Confederate States, we cannot attach to it the same value that you do; a mere inferential recognition unconnected with political action *or the regular establishment of diplomatic relations* possessing none of the moral weight required for awakening the people of the U. S. from their delusion that these States still remain members of the old Union. Nothing will end this war but the utter exhaustion of the belligerents, unless by the action of some of the leading powers of Europe in entering into formal relations with us, the United States are made to perceive that we are in the eyes of the world a separate nation.... This letter shows that his address to the President as 'President of the Confederate States' is a formula of politeness to his correspondent, *not* a political recognition of a fact. None of our political journals treat the letter as a *recognition* in the sense you attach to it."

It was a cruel disillusionment, after all Mann's efforts and hopes.

But the priceless document he had obtained from the Pope was not destined to be wholly lost. A generation later a visitor to Jefferson Davis's home in New Orleans was shown by that statesman's daughter a framed parchment hanging on the wall.

"One of dear papa's most valued souvenirs," she explained, wiping the dust which had gathered upon the glass.

ALTHOUGH Slidell was aware of the extent to which European emigration to the Northern states for service with the Union armies was encouraged, and the large sums spent on emigration propaganda in Germany, Russia, Italy, France (especially Alsace) and Belgium, his own efforts were greatly limited, largely owing to the difficulty of transport. But during 1864 considerable numbers of able-bodied men applied to him for facilities to reach Havana or Matamoras with the design of joining the Confederate army, among whom were numerous Polish exiles. In June he received a visit from two Poles, one a Colonel Smolenski who had formerly lived in Texas, and the other, named Buymicki, whose property had been seized by the Russian authorities and his wife sent to Siberia. They were accompanied by one Williams, an Englishman, secretary of the Anglo-Polish league, who unfolded an ambitious scheme. It aimed at colonising the northern frontier states of the Confederacy, such as Virginia, Kentucky and Tennessee, by large bodies of Poles who with their families were to be offered a passage and free lands on condition of their bearing arms in defence of their homes. The first were forthcoming; recruiting stations would at once be opened in Paris. The Confederate Commissioner thought the plan would have the support of his Government, and with this encouragement Colonel Smolenski set about recruiting his fellow-countrymen, who had refused all offers to go to the United States on account of its reputed alliance with Russia. Already a similar number had been collected at Liverpool and were on the point of sailing, and there were other parties in readiness in Switzerland and Italy.

On getting wind of all this, Bigelow complained to the Prefect of Police to put a check on Smolenski's recruiting activities, so far as Paris was concerned, and this was promptly done.

The Federal Government, on the other hand, had no need to mention recruiting; the hard times in Europe made hundreds of thousands of English, Irish, Germans, Scandinavians and Italians ready to cross the sea in the hope of any sort of a living. On their arrival in New York or Boston they were quickly snapped up by recruiting agents or drafted willy-nilly into the army. Generally they had no objection to military service if they were well paid for it, and to them the soldier's pay was very high. In the second year of the conflict, Secretary Seward prepared a circular to all his diplomatic agents abroad calling the world's attention to "what deserves to be regarded as one of the most important steps ever taken by any Government toward a practical recognition of the universal brotherhood of nations." This, in other words, was the Homestead Act of 1861, offering 160 acres free to any and all comers who would agree to occupy them, scattered over sixteen States and two million square miles of territory. The Consul General in Paris had this document printed broadcast over the Continent and afterwards complacently remarked upon "the light that it throws upon the mysterious repletion of our army during the four years of War, while it was notoriously being so fearfully depleted by fire-arms, disease and desertion."

CHAPTER VIII
A DREAM OF MEXICO

NAPOLEON III had long been interested in Mexico, that tropical land doomed to perpetual bloody revolutions, clerical intrigues and foreign exploiters, of which John Slidell had been an official spectator in 1845.

"I was fully persuaded," wrote a distinguished Southerner, M. F. Maury, to Secretary Benjamin, recalling a lengthy interview with the Emperor in 1860, "that he proposed to seek in Mexico a compensation for the lost Colonies in the West Indies which, he said, could not be recovered *sans nous brouiller avec nos alliés*. He insisted that France must sooner or later have a *pied-à-terre* on the Florida coast for the purpose of protecting her commerce in the Gulf, for, he added, '*Nous ne voulons pas un autre Gibraltar de ce côte-la.*'"

Two or three years later it seemed as if Mexico might prove the touchstone which would decide the fate of the Confederacy. For when the first gun was fired at Sumter and North and South were engaged, the Monroe Doctrine was in abeyance and Europe's chance to interfere in the affairs of the Western Hemisphere synchronised with a definite provocation. This came from the Mexican Dictator, Benito Juarez, who has, in the twentieth century, gained an additional posthumous celebrity as "the other Benito."

"The origin of the present Mexican imbroglio," explained Slidell to a correspondent in the early autumn of 1863, "dates from the *coup,* three years ago, of the Swiss banker, Jecker, who lent President Miramon the sum of $750,000. For this he appears to have received bonds for twenty times that sum. When Juarez came into power he declined to recognise Jecker's claim except for the actual money lent. The creditor came to Paris and laid his affair before the Duc de Morny, who perceived great political and commercial possibilities in the business. Jecker became a French subject and the Emperor, who has long had his eye on Mexico, needed little inducement to espouse his interests. That country was already giving umbrage to England and Spain by shooting their subjects and not paying their debts and this led to the tripartite convention of 1861, and the despatch of an allied force to teach the Mexicans to mend their ways."

Somebody or other has always been trying to teach the Mexicans to mend their ways. Will those Mexican ways—one is sometimes tempted to ask—never be mended?

What caused England and Spain to break off in Mexico and come home was a suspicion of France's ulterior designs. For not only Jecker and Co. but a large number of Mexican refugees, especially the clerics, had got the ear of the Emperor—or at least of the Empress—and persuaded both that the revival of monarchy in Mexico was the only means of stabilising the country.

Even before the London Convention, the French Foreign Minister, Thouvenel, had written to Flahault, the Ambassador in London (September, 1861):

> "Is the Government of the Latin races possible except under the monarchical form? I do not believe it is, and I am assured that all the honest and sensible people in Mexico are of that opinion."

In order to prove his disinterestedness, the Emperor was prepared to engage himself to decline the candidature of any French prince.

> "I am," continued Thouvenel, "altogether of your opinion about the reception which the United States would probably give our proposition, and that in my

opinion we would only have to regulate our relations with them without awaiting their co-operation. They have at present other cats to whip than the Mexicans; and it seems to me impossible that the question of Cotton should not within three months from this time put England and France under the necessity of consulting before all an interest vital to the prosperity and repose of their industrial cities."

It was natural that his desire for a predominating influence in Mexico should have further inclined Napoleon to favour the success of the Confederates. On the face of it, the Mexican Empire (or the French Empire in Mexico) would stand a better chance against two rival Republics than against one "individual democratic Union pledged to resist European interference with the balance of power in the Western Hemisphere." From the Confederate point of view a French army in Mexico and free transportation of contraband goods was an alluring prospect; besides, the privilege of Franco-Mexican ships to convoy much-needed cargoes into Wilmington and Charleston was an important consideration.

But from a further secret despatch of Thouvenel's to London (January 17, 1862), it would appear that it was not intended that the Confederacy, even if successful, should acquire any footing in Mexico, and also that Napoleon was already advanced in his plans for a future Mexican monarchy.

Upon the retirement of the British and Spanish, a very large force of French troops was sent out, and thus France found herself heavily committed to the Mexican adventure.

After much manœuvring and several awkward reverses the French army entered Mexico City on June 17, 1863, and shortly afterwards a Provisional Government, nominated by Dubois de Saligny, the French minister plenipotentiary, was set up. The principle of a monarchy being approved, an invitation was addressed to the Austrian Archduke Maximilian to occupy the throne. This blameless young man, who had married the daughter of Leopold I of Belgium, had retired from the Austrian navy and was living with his bride, his books and his pictures in the charming villa, "Miramar," on the shores of the Adriatic.

Matters had reached this stage when in October, 1863, there turned up at Slidell's office in Paris a gentleman whose card was inscribed "James De Haviland."

He recalled himself to Slidell's memory as a former visitor to Washington, an English author and traveller. It appeared that he knew Mexico intimately—repeating the word "intimately"—so that Slidell, who had only gazed at Mexico for several months, from afar— may have scented an affront. But De Haviland's sympathies were, as he sought to assure Slidell, with the South and, being then on his way to Austria, he intended visiting the Archduke Maximilian and ascertaining from him if possible, his sentiments towards the Confederacy. Slidell received this intimation coldly: the English visitor was bowed out and forgotten. A few weeks later, there came from him the following letter, dated from Trieste:

"Having recently been honoured with an invitation to Miramar, H. I. H. the Archduke yesterday favoured me with a long private interview during which he expressed the warmest possible interest in the success of the Confederate cause. He said that he considered it identical with that of the new Mexican Empire—in fact so inseparable that an acknowledgment of the Confederate States of America by the Governments of England and France should take place *before* his acceptance of the Mexican crown became unconditional; that he was particularly desirous that his sentiments upon this subject should be known to the Confederate President and to the statesmen and leading minds of the Confederacy, and authorised me confidentially to communicate these views to President Davis and to you, Sir, and

also to make known to both of you the solicitude
with which he was watching the present movements
of the Confederate army."

This, if genuine, was a highly important disclosure.
But Slidell doubted its genuineness; he suspected De
Haviland of being a Yankee emissary and was on his
guard. He instructed his secretary Eustis merely to
acknowledge it and to say that he would confer with
the Mexican Minister, Señor Gutierrez de Estrada, to
whom De Haviland had referred him.

Slidell called promptly on Gutierrez, who admitted
having introduced De Haviland to the Archduke and
stated his belief in his *bona fides*.

> "I allowed M. Gutierrez," reported Slidell to Ben-
> jamin, "at his request to take a copy of the letter that
> he might send it to Miramar, authorising him to
> state confidentially the suspicions I entertain of the
> writer and to hint the propriety of employing some
> other channel of communication."

For a fortnight Slidell heard nothing further.

A friend at the Quai d'Orsay, however, confirmed
what De Haviland had stated of the value that the
Archduke attached to French recognition of the Confederacy. He had "seen the paper in which the Archduke set forth the different measures which he

considers essential to the successful establishment of his Government; the recognition of the Confederacy headed the list."

Slidell now sent a copy of De Haviland's letter to Drouyn de Lhuys, then at Compiègne. "Some of the French papers," he wrote to Benjamin, "alluding to rumours in circulation, deny that the Archduke insists upon the recognition of the Confederacy and speak of his acceptance of the Mexican crown as certain. For myself in the present condition of affairs I consider it very doubtful."

De Haviland's letter was duly shown to the Emperor Napoleon, who was visibly annoyed by it and took immediate steps to inform his protégé, Maximilian, of the embarrassing character of such statements at that critical moment. Thus rebuked, the Archduke declared that the letter was wholly misleading and misrepresented the facts of his interview with De Haviland. But what he resented more particularly was Slidell's interference; and it certainly seemed as if Slidell might have been more discreet in the use he made of De Haviland's letter to force the Emperor's hand.

Whether, however, he went so far as Bigelow, on the authority of General Preston, stated he did, is hardly likely. According to this story—Slidell, "while playing at the [Union] club one night with Persigny and De Morny, among others, stated what he had learned through De Haviland about a certain promise in high quarters.

"One of the dukes—for in those days it was the fashion to call Persigny and De Morny both 'Duke' —said that Maximilian had never made any such request. Slidell reaffirmed his statement. The duke repeated in yet more emphatic terms that it was not true. Slidell rose from his seat and with some vehemence exclaimed, 'By God, no man whether duke or Emperor, shall say that John Slidell ever said what was not true!' Of course, the offending, and on that account, if for no better reason, offended party, duly, promptly took his revenge upon the intemperate diplomatist by reporting his language to the Emperor, by whom it was very naturally construed as an impeachment of his Majesty's veracity.

"When, subsequently, Slidell applied for an audience with the Emperor the application was granted, but no time was fixed. A further application was made for a designation of the time. After two or three days' delay Slidell was informed that the note granting the audience was withdrawn; in other words that he had no longer any standing at the court to which he was accredited."

Commenting on this, Bigelow gives free rein to his powers of reprobation.

"Imagine Dr. Franklin allowing himself to be beguiled into association where, to maintain his self-respect, he is constrained to insult the Government which it was the vital concern of his mission to conciliate!

"An insane idea of his own importance, aggravated by the anxieties of the gaming-table, made Slidell lose sight entirely of the great trust which had been confided to him, and place it as well as himself at the mercy of the two most conspicuous and reckless adventurers in Europe."

This is picturesquely said, but is hardly justified. While it is probable that an incident of the sort described happened and Slidell really lost his temper with the Duc de Morny, yet we have the best of reasons for disbelieving in the alleged consequences, as far as Napoleon was concerned. The latter well knew that Maximilian was trying, as a hundred others had tried, to force his hand, about recognising the Confederacy and that Slidell had been made use of for this purpose. Consequently, he felt no resentment whatever. The case was different with Maximilian, who had encountered Morny's opposition to the Mexican adventure and was now being persuaded that his true interest lay in keeping silence about his Southern sympathies. He felt annoyed with both De Haviland and Slidell: but no direct intimation of his annoyance appears to have reached the Confederate Commissioner in Paris.

Slidell attached great importance to the Mexican Empire if it ever came into being. It was unfortunate there was so much delay in getting it started. When he saw Drouyn de Lhuys on February 19th that statesman "manifested great dissatisfaction at the tardiness of the Archduke's movements and said that he ought then to be far on his way to Mexico."

> "I think," reported Slidell, "there is a great anxiety to see him embark, and thus so completely committed as to render it impossible to further exaggerate the unpopularity of the Mexican expedition among all classes and parties in France. It is the only subject upon which the public opinion seems to be unanimous. I have yet to meet the first man who approves of it, and several persons near the Emperor have spoken to me of it in decided terms of condemnation."

He thought the Emperor was fully aware of this feeling and wanted to get rid of the embarrassment as soon as he decently could.

> "The Archduke may be obliged to rely on his own resources at a much earlier day than he expects. In this opinion I may perhaps do the Emperor injustice, but I cannot otherwise account for the evidently

increased desire to avoid giving umbrage to the Lincoln Government."

At last, however, it was announced that the future Emperor had arrived at Brussels on a visit to his father-in-law, King Leopold, and would immediately afterwards come to Paris en route for the seat of his future Empire.

> "We are expecting the Archduke in a few days," reported Slidell at the end of February. "He is to stay at the Tuileries and there are to be many festivities which I trust will not interfere with our coming at last to a full personal understanding of his policy towards us."

On March 3rd, 1864, he was disgusted by a telegram from Brussels to say that his Imperial Highness had cancelled his Paris engagements. Rumour ran that the cautious Leopold had advised him "not to put his foot in France, much less in Mexico, unless the Emperor will support him in case of difficulty with the United States."

For Napoleon to take any step of this kind would certainly have been politically imprudent. The watchful Corps Legislatif was in session, and there was scant sympathy in that quarter for the Mexican scheme.

The Paris visit was, however, only postponed for a

few days. Maximilian duly appeared. On the very day of his arrival Slidell despatched a message to Gutierrez de Estrada expressing a desire to see his Imperial Highness on important business. An answer was returned that the Archduke would be pleased to see him and that an appointment would forthwith be made by his secretary.

Days passed and no word came. Slidell grew anxious, especially as it was announced that the royal visit would only last a week. He wrote to the secretary, enclosing M. Gutierrez's note and again begging an audience. In vain—no answer came.

> "I am told," explained Slidell, "that as regards this apparent discourtesy I had no cause to complain, as the applications for audiences had been so numerous as to make it impossible to answer any of them. Be this as it may, I considered the refusal or rather the avoiding of the Archduke to hear what I had to say as very significant, as it may fairly be presumed that my application had not been overlooked, but that he had considered it inexpedient to see me. This presumption is strengthened by a fact which I have heard from a reliable source."

On March 22 Slidell wrote again:

> "I yesterday saw General Woll, the first aide-de-camp of the future Emperor who goes out with him

in the *Novara;* he left last evening for Miramar. He
is the only Frenchman who accompanies him and
probably will be the only person on board thoroughly acquainted with Mexico and well posted as
regards the Yankees and the Confederacy. *I have
talked to him very freely as to the consequences that
will result from a refusal to be on good terms with
the Confederacy."*

Slidell could always take a high tone when his pride
was wounded.

Meanwhile, a thousand leagues away, in consequence of the sentiments expressed by Maximilian to
De Haviland, the Richmond Government had appointed a Minister Plenipotentiary and Envoy Extraordinary to the Imperial Court of Mexico. Their
choice had fallen upon a robust and genial Kentuckian,
General William Preston, who had formerly been
United States Minister to Spain. This gallant warrior
had proceeded no farther on his mission than Havana
when some doubts arose in his mind as to his reception
by the Emperor Maximilian and he thought it prudent to send an emissary to Mexico to ascertain the true
position of affairs. Such a course was always advisable
in the case of Mexico, as Slidell could have told him.
Preston also reflected that "it was not consistent with
the dignity of the Government he represented to send

a representative to the Court of Maximilian before a representative of that Court had been accredited."

The messenger upon whom Preston now relied was a certain Dr. William Gwin, a Southerner and a former Federal Senator, who had thrown himself heart and soul into a grandiose scheme for establishing a model colony in Mexico, to be called Sonora. Gwin was convinced that the country back of Guaymas was richer in gold and silver than California itself. He had gone to Paris and unfolded his maps and exhibited his mineralogical specimens to the Emperor, who was enchanted. The Finance Minister, Fould, had suggested the granting of large mining monopolies to certain French corporations for the development and colonisation of Sonora. But Gwin insisted upon exploitation solely by private enterprise and was confident that he could induce fifteen or twenty thousand experienced California miners to take up claims in the country. The Emperor approved of this, in spite of Fould's opposition. The views of Maximilian were consulted and he, likewise agreeing, Gwin was forthwith appointed Governor of the new district of Sonora. Napoleon furnished him with a letter to the local commander of the French forces, thereby insuring the military protection of the expected settlers and the expulsion of hostile Indians.

As Preston wrote Slidell, Gwin in leaving Havana had expressed himself as most anxious to secure friendly relations between Mexico and the Confederacy, because "the success of his scheme will depend upon the emigration of Southern men from California. He was afraid from what he had heard at Paris that attempts to establish intercourse would be abandoned by me, and he is very earnest in urging the necessity of action and recognition at once by Maximilian."

Preston was confident that Gwin would procure an invitation for him to proceed to Mexico within a short time.

> "He is to urge the general arguments with all the force he can command and secure the opportune delivery of certain letters I have written to the Marquis de Montholon and General Almonte, privately. I am to withdraw from Havana for a time, so that the danger of other arrangements or the possibility of engrafting the Monroe doctrine in the treaty of peace, in case of rebuff, may awaken the Emperor to the rights of the Confederacy and the dangers of delay."

While he was waiting at Havana Preston received from Slidell an account of the shabby manner in which he had just been treated by the Archduke and also of the return to Paris of Mercier, the French Minister at

Washington, who, more fortunate than himself, had actually been accorded an interview with the Archduke.

Mercier, so Slidell further reported, had declared that at his parting interview with President Lincoln in Washington he had been

> "authorised to say to the Archduke that his Government would be recognised by that of Washington without difficulty, *on the condition, however, that no negotiations should be entered into with the Confederate States.*
>
> "This assurance, repeated to the Archduke by M. Mercier, has probably influenced his course towards me; and he is weak and credulous enough to think he can keep on good terms with the Yankees, while he can at any time in case of need, command the *friendship and support of the Confederacy.*"

Slidell continued:

> "I have taken care, of course in no offensive terms, to let the leading Mexicans here understand that he makes a great mistake, both as regards his hope of avoiding difficulties with the North and his reliance upon the South to aid him in meeting them should they occur; that without the actual friendship of the South he will be entirely powerless to resist Northern aggression, while he, in his turn, can render us no

service in the present or any future war with the
North; that our motive in desiring to negotiate with
Mexico was not the expectation of desiring any advantage from an alliance *per se,* but from the consequences that would probably flow from it in another
quarter; that when we should have conquered peace,
while we would desire to be on friendly terms with
all nations, we should have no special interest in the
stability of the Mexican Government, and would be
free to pursue such a policy as circumstances and our
interest might dictate."

As a matter of fact, while we now know that Minister Mercier had no farewell audience with Lincoln,
yet in a conversation with Chase, Secretary of the
Treasury, he was told that "the United States would
not interfere against Mexico, if France did not recognise the Confederate States." No matter who expressed
this sentiment, it is clear enough that it represented the
views of the Washington Government.

> "Now that you know what has occurred here,"
> wrote Slidell to Preston, while the latter was still
> waiting in Havana, "you can decide whether you
> will at once proceed to Mexico or take measures to
> ascertain in advance what reception you are likely to
> meet with by the new Government there."

But the Confederate envoy had already decided to
clear out of Cuba for a time. He planned to return in

September to receive the hoped-for invitation at the hands of Dr. Gwin.

"I am," Preston wrote,* "surrounded by many embarrassments, but will steadily endeavour to accomplish your wishes. I think we will obtain recognition at Mexico as soon or sooner than at any other court. The mighty contest at Richmond, more filled with great results to mankind than any of the present century, or perhaps the past, will decide everything. The dreadful repulses of Grant will end in rout, or, at most, an inglorious and weary siege. I wait for and believe in a triumph of our arms so dazzling that all Governments and Monarchs will throw open their courts for our welcome. My situation here for the last four months has been exceedingly disagreeable. The Captain-General, though professing sympathy for the Confederacy, is really afraid of the North. The recent outrage in the extradition of Colonel Arguelles by the Lincoln government rendered him still more supple. I cannot expect, in the slowness of Mexican communication, any definite information before September, and, for the reasons I have stated, I will go to Europe on the steamer sailing direct to Liverpool tomorrow, and return in time to get Doctor Gwin's and Captain Ford's intelligence and replies from the Marquis de Montholon and General Almonte for my guidance. I

* To Jefferson Davis, June 28, 1864.

will see Mr. Mason and Mr. Slidell, and be in Europe in a fortnight."

General Preston had only been in the French capital a few hours when he received an unexpected visit from M. Mercier, who expressed to him his deep interest in the cause both of the Confederacy (which he had lately journeyed through) and of Mexico. He strongly advised Preston to call upon the Emperor at Compiègne and offered to make the necessary arrangements, if Preston would forward the customary application to the Grand Chamberlain. Whereupon the General observed that he could only ask or receive such a privilege through the diplomatic agent of his Government.

"In that case," said Mercier, "you will only meet with failure, as Mr. Slidell is now *persona non grata* to his Majesty."

He then related the story of the incident at the club and Slidell's alleged fatal loss of temper.

Preston, however, was by no means satisfied with Mercier's own attitude, and when he came to talk with Slidell he felt more dubious than ever. Mercier had repeatedly assured Slidell that he was confident that the Lincoln policy concerning Mexico would be carried out. Slidell's own comment on this was: "Unwilling to admit himself to have been duped, he naturally endeavours to impress that opinion upon others."

He began to change his view of Mercier's character. He had formerly believed him to have "strong sympathies with our cause and that any influence he could exercise would be in our favour. I have now good reason to believe that desiring to be 'all things to all men' he avows Northern or Southern preferences as he may suppose the expression of the one or the other will be most agreeable to those with whom he converses."

Slidell's failure with Maximilian, as related in the Paris Commissioner's despatches, made a bad impression on the Government at Richmond.

"It had long been foreseen by us," commented Secretary Benjamin in a burst of patriotic rhapsody, "that Mr. Seward would hesitate at no promises in order to postpone the evil day which is approaching with such giant strides, when the whole structure of the North will topple from its sandy foundation, and our recognition be forced not only upon neutrals but upon the enemy by the strength, valour and fortitude of our people. Every hour produces fresh evidence of the early and disastrous breakdown in Northern resources, both of men and money, and our day of happy deliverance is seen to be dawning by those even who have hitherto been despondent.

The contrast between our armies and those of the
enemy in dash, spirit and confidence is amazing and
is displayed so strikingly as to produce a marked effect on the spirit of the people in the two countries.
You cannot fail to be impressed with the wonderful
change in the tone of the public journals North and
South. But Europe is still as blind as ever and hugs
with fondness the delusive promises of the U. S.
Secretary of State; and if it be true that the conduct
of the Archduke has been influenced by the Emperor,
and that the latter in turn has been influenced by Mr.
Seward, the absence of the sagacity that has therefore
characterised the Imperial policy is indeed remarkable. It is therefore difficult to believe that the Emperor can have leaned on so feeble a reed as the
promises made by the Northern Cabinet; a reed
which has already been broken and pierced his hand,
as shown by the unanimous vote of the House of
Representatives on the subject of Maximilian's recognition."

All this is in Benjamin's best forensic style. He continues:

"The fact, however, of the silence of the Archduke
and his sudden departure from Paris, after the previous interchange of his views with us through
unofficial communications, and the conduct of the
French Government in detaining the *Rappahannock,*
are indications of a submission to Northern dictation

similar to that which has marked the course of the British Cabinet and inflicted on us wrongs which have exasperated our people almost beyond the limits of endurance. It is therefore with extreme solicitude that we await the answer of the Government to your demand in relation to the *Rappahannock*. If it should be unfavourable, my own impression is that we should not only pursue without hesitation the course indicated by you of striking her flag and leaving her to the disposal of the French Government on its responsibility, but that we should secure ourselves adequate indemnity by *seizing and detaining the French tobacco here*. My only fear is that the news from you on this subject will arrive too late to enable us to give full effect to such a measure, as the *French ships are now taking the tobacco,* and may be *ready to depart* before receipt of your next despatch."

But it was not too late and the French Government was punished by having the tobacco, purchased by their merchants in Virginia, impounded, an act "justified on grounds entirely independent of any retaliatory spirit.... We have thus been enabled to show that there were French interests as dependent on our good will as we are on that of the Emperor's Government."

The Richmond Government continued very sore, and Benjamin did not mince his words.

"We cannot," he wrote Slidell (June 23rd, 1864), "resist the conclusion that there has been bad faith and deception in the course pursued by the Emperor, who has not hesitated to break his promises to us in order to escape the consequences resulting from his unpopular Mexican policy.

"The game played by the Cabinet of the United States with the French Government in relation to Mexico is so transparent that the inference is irresistible that the latter desire to be deceived. The acceptance by Mr. Lincoln of his nomination by the Baltimore Convention commits him openly to refusing acknowledgment of the Mexican Empire, and the platform of that convention, of the Cleveland Convention which nominated Frémont, and the platform which will undoubtedly be adopted by the Democratic Convention at Chicago show a feeling in the United States perfectly unanimous in the determination to overthrow the schemes of the French Government in Mexico, and to resist the occupation of the throne by Maximilian. It has thus become evident that the safety of the new Empire is dependent solely upon *our* success in interposing a barrier between Northern aggression and the Mexican territory.

"As we do not intend to allow ourselves to be made use of in this matter as a convenient instrument for the accomplishment of the designs of others, you will not be surprised to learn the nature of the last instructions sent to Mr. Preston, of which a copy is annexed."

That was not all. Recent utterances of French Ministers indicated an *entente* between the Cabinets of Washington and Paris so that

"we should be blind indeed if we failed to attach to these incidents their true significance. We feel therefore the necessity of receiving with extreme distrust any assurances whatever that may emanate from a party capable of the double dealing displayed towards us by the Imperial Government.

"Our military position is promising in the extreme, and I do not think I go too far in saying that the Federal Campaign of 1864 is already a failure. We may meet with reverses, but nothing at present indicates any danger comparable with the menacing aspect of affairs prior to the success of our noble army in repulsing the repeated and desperate assaults of the Federal armies with a slaughter perfectly appalling."

But the Federal campaign soon proved itself anything but a failure, and Slidell, when in September he met the Emperor at the races in the Bois de Boulogne, was hard put to it to minimise the effect of Sherman's triumphant march to the sea:

"... I met the Emperor; he recognised me at some distance and came towards me, greeting me very cordially with a shake of the hand. He inquired if I had been well, and asked if I had received from the Minister of War notice of an order for the admission of my son at St. Cyr. I said that I had to thank him very sincerely for his kindness in affording my son an opportunity of acquiring a good military education. He replied that it was quite unnecessary, as he was pleased to have an opportunity of showing his good-will. I have not before alluded to this circumstance because an order had not been actually given, although the Emperor had very promptly promised M. de Persigny to grant the permission on his application made about the 10th instant, and indeed I should not probably have mentioned the matter officially had I not had occasion to report my conversation with the Emperor.

"The Emperor, after making enquiries about my family, asked me what I thought of our military position, especially in Georgia, and of the effect of the fall of Atlanta. I said I was happy to assure him that the abandonment of Atlanta was a much less serious matter than was generally supposed in Europe, as we had removed all the valuable machinery and material weeks before Sherman took possession; that the only effect of Sherman's advance was to increase the distance from his base of supplies and make his communications more liable to interruption; that I did not think it at all improbable that we should soon hear of his falling back upon

Chattanooga. He asked if the report of the surrender of Mobile was true. I said that I was confident not only that the report was premature, but that we should be able to hold Mobile as we had Charleston."

Thus did Slidell continue to hug the bright illusion to his bosom.

"I went on to say that we might soon expect stirring news from the armies near Petersburg, and I doubted not that Lee would give a good account of Grant. He expressed his admiration and astonishment at what he had achieved against such enormous odds, and his confidence in our ability to maintain ourselves; he spoke of the impossibility of occupying a territory like ours, and his regret that our many victories had not been followed by more decisive results. I answered that this was susceptible of easy explanation; that we were always fighting against superior numbers and had no strong reserves to follow up our successes; that the troops that had been engaged were generally exhausted by fatigue; that our great battles had usually been a series of desperate fighting for several days, and while we had inflicted much heavier losses on the enemy, we had necessarily been much crippled ourselves. Besides, our cavalry, from the difficulty of renewing our stock of horses, was much less numerous and efficient than it had been, and we were unable to pursue and harass a beaten and retreating enemy with such effect as would be expected in Europe under similar circumstances.

"The Emperor asked me what were the prospects of peace. I replied that had the question been put to me ten days before I should have replied that they were good, but that the letter of McClellan accepting the Democratic nomination for the presidency had completely dissipated them; that Lincoln would probably be re-elected, and that the war would be continued until a revolution should break out in the free states. I asked him if he had read McClellan's letter; he said that he had, that it had greatly disappointed him, for he had entertained strong hope that the terrible conflict would soon be ended. He then left me with another cordial shake of the hand.

"A year ago I should have attached some important political signification to this incident; as it is I merely consider it as indicating personal kind feeling towards the representative of a cause that commands his respect and good wishes."

In truth, Slidell's sincerest feeling had found vent in a letter to Mason of two months before.

"The time has now arrived when it is comparatively of very little importance what Queen or Emperor may say or think about us. A plague, I say, on both your houses." *

* July 17, 1864.

CHAPTER IX

THE STRANGE CASE OF MINISTER DAYTON

THE *Alabama!* It is hard for the present generation, even helped by the memory of the exploits of
the German *Goeben* in the World War, to realise what
that name meant on the high seas in 1864, and especially to American shipping. Famous as it was, it was
destined to become more famous still, when an august
legal assembly gathered together at Geneva to examine, denounce and assess its sinister prowess, and
today the *Alabama* stands as a landmark in the annals of international jurisprudence. But by that time
the hull of this almost legendary ship was rotting or
rusting fathoms deep in the English Channel.

On the 12th of June, 1864, the rumour spread in
Paris, especially in naval, seafaring and diplomatic circles, amongst journalists and American partisans, that
the dreaded *Alabama,* Confederate corsair, had entered the port of Cherbourg. To use her intrepid com-

mander's words, she resembled "a weary foxhound, limping back after a long chase, footsore and longing for quiet and repose." She had been at sea incessantly for two years, always on the alert, with no friendly port wherein to lay her head, with no rest for her boilers, whose fires were always banked, and small chance for cleaning and repairs. Much of her cruising had been in the tropics, but those were periods amidst heat of the equator, the blazing suns of Malacca and the China sea. Such vicissitudes of climate were alone enough to test her endurance. But in addition "the wear and tear of such a cruise, such a lengthened period of restless activity, with no means to supply deficiencies or to repair injuries, except what might be found in captured vessels, told upon the little craft at last." Rounding the Cape of Good Hope, her commander, Captain Semmes, early in this year, worked leisurely up through the sea routes, capturing an occasional prize, but finding few now in his path, for there were few who dared to venture forth. So, on the 11th June, he brought his tired sea-dog into Cherbourg, hoping that the French authorities would allow him to refit.

Immediately the American Consul telegraphed the news to Paris. The American Minister, Dayton, might have exclaimed piously, "Lord, thou hast delivered

mine enemy into my hands!" For the United States
warship, *Kearsarge,* Captain John A. Winslow, lay at
Flushing, armed and equipped, waiting for just such
a chance to grapple with the enemy. A message was at
once sent to him to come round to Cherbourg, where
it was not believed Semmes would be permitted to remain long. On his arrival Semmes had landed a number of Federal prisoners and these Captain Winslow
promptly demanded should be allowed to join the
Kearsarge. This was, of course, refused by the French
port authorities. Winslow then, without anchor-
ing, took up a waiting position outside the breakwater.

Parties from Paris now arrived daily at Cherbourg,
Eustis and Vignaud amongst them, to greet the valiant Semmes. Dayton sent his son to confer with and
support the local United States Consul. There was a
crowd of journalists and a number of naval and military officers. For by this time it was known that the
Kearsarge intended to offer battle to the *Alabama* the
moment she left the port. It became a question with
Captain Semmes whether he should wait to complete
his repairs and then attempt to steal out on a dark
night, as he had often done before, or go out at once
openly and engage his Federal antagonist.

The two cruisers were not ill-matched both as re-

From a painting by Manet

The Alabama and the Kearsage

gards tonnage * and armament: and, apart from the fresher condition of the *Kearsarge,* it seemed simply a question of crew and marksmanship.

The Federal ship carried four 32-pound guns in broadside, two 11-inch Dahlgram guns pivoted on deck and one 28-pound rifled gun, pivoted on the topgallant forecastle.

As for the *Alabama,* she had six 32-pounders in broadside, instead of her original eight, and one 7-inch 100-pound rifled gun, pivoted. It was therefore a fair match. Superiority in seamanship would be difficult to demonstrate: their spread being equal, all might depend on the conditions under which the impending battle was fought.

What troubled Semmes more than anything else was that his crew had been deprived of target practice. Brave and disciplined as they were, they had from the first, owing to a chronic shortage of ordnance, lacked that proper training in gunnery which gives men coolness, skill in judging distances, and precision of aim. Only once or twice had the *Alabama's* battery been brought into play, as in the brief engagement with the *Hatteras.* Nevertheless, he hoped for the best. He notified his waiting opponent, through the American Con-

---

* The *Alabama's* tonnage was 1,040: her length 220 feet; her engines were about 1,000 horsepower.

sul, that he would come out and fight him as soon as he had finished coaling.

At half-past nine on the morning of the 19th of June the *Alabama* got under way and steamed out of Cherbourg harbour, to the cheering of the crowd assembled on shore. Later in the day numbers repaired to the hills about Cherbourg, equipped with telescopes; while a daring few ventured out in yachts and tugs. Yet it was hardly the case, as Admiral Farragut wrote admiringly his son that "the battle was fought like a tournament, in full view of thousands of French and English," and that "people came from Paris to witness the fight."

> "As a matter of fact [comments Captain Bulloch, who, however, arrived too late to see the fight], not a score of people knew from a Confederate source that the engagement would take place, or when, and the 'thousands of French and English' who are said to have witnessed it, must have been either the floating and idle population of a seaport, the majority of whom probably did not know one ship from the other, or they were persons who get their information from the United States Consul, and who were therefore hopeful, if not confident, that the *Kearsarge* would win. There were a few naval officers who went to the best points of observation with the expectation that there would be an opportunity to take some interesting and useful notes; but as the

ships steamed away from the land some seven miles to get well beyond the 'line of jurisdiction' before the action began, but little of the effect could have been seen."

At seven miles out the *Kearsarge's* prow turned sharply around and steered towards the *Alabama*. Both ships cleared for action, with batteries pivoted to starboard. When they were about a mile apart, the *Alabama* opened fire. Three broadsides followed in succession, but aimed so high as only to damage her opponent's rigging.

The ships drew nearer together: at a thousand yards the guns of the *Kearsarge* responded and the firing became active, the distance gradually lessening to four hundred yards.

It was soon realised that gunnery was to be the decisive factor in the battle. Semmes, recognising his inferiority in this respect, tried to manœuvre closer to his adversary: the two ships continued steaming at full speed opposite each other, but describing a circular course. The *Alabama* received terrible punishment almost from the first. At least twenty 11-inch shells crashed into her sides and through her decks. A large proportion of the 173 shot and shells fired by the *Kearsarge* gunners must have found their mark.

Far otherwise was the effect of the *Alabama's* bom-

bardment. It was not altogether a case of bad marksmanship. Even when a direct hit was scored upon her
adversary the damage was comparatively slight. Once
a 7-inch shell lodged in the stern-post of the *Kearsarge*
—the most vital point in the vessel. If it had exploded
it would have shattered the wood-ends which form the
counter of the hull and the ship would probably have
foundered. But it did not explode. Twenty-eight times
did such shells strike the enemy, but the only damage
was to a couple of longboats. The *Alabama's* powder
had deteriorated through being kept too long in a bad
climate and also in the wrong place on board.

Captain Semmes wrote afterwards:

> "Perceiving that our shells, though apparently ex-
> ploding against the enemy's sides, were doing him
> but little damage, I returned to solid-shot firing;
> and several naval experts who witnessed the engage-
> ment from the hills near Cherbourg have told me
> that they were struck with the difference in the ap-
> pearance of the flame and smoke produced by the
> explosions of the shells from the two ships. Those
> from the *Kearsarge* emitted a quick bright flash, and
> the smoke went quickly away in a fine blue vapour,
> while those from the *Alabama* exhaled a dull flame
> and a mass of sluggish grey smoke."

Moreover, the *Kearsarge* was protected amidships
by the steel chain cables which were stowed outside,

STRANGE CASE OF MINISTER DAYTON 239

hanging vertically so as to cover the engine space, thus forming a sort of armour-plate for her most vital parts. Semmes, in his report, says that the officers whom he sent to the *Kearsarge* with the wounded, informed him that the covering boards had been ripped off in many directions, and in some places the chains had been broken and forced partly into the ship's side by the *Alabama's* shot and shells. "If those projectiles had found their way into that protected section of the *Kearsarge,* the engagement might have had a different result."

But about the result there was soon no doubt. With her hull riddled with shells, one hole near the waterline, "through which a barrel might have been passed," with nine men killed and twenty-one wounded, the thrilling and adventurous career of the *Alabama* was over. George Eustis on shore saw her slowly subside into the waters of the Channel. Captain Semmes made a desperate effort to approach the French coast by ekeing out the dying efforts of her engines with the fore-and-aft sails; but it was too late. A last raking broadside from her adversary and the *coup de grâce* had been delivered.

"The ship filled so rapidly, however, that before we had made much progress, the fires were extinguished in the furnaces, and we were evidently on the point of sinking. I now hauled down my colours, to prevent the further destruction of life, and despatched a boat to inform the enemy of our condition. Although we were now but 400 yards from each other, the enemy fired upon me five times after my colours had been struck. It is charitable to suppose that a ship of war of a Christian nation could not have done this intentionally. We now directed all our exertions toward saving the wounded and such of the boys of the ship as were unable to swim. These were despatched in my quarter-boats, the only boats remaining to me; the waist-boats having been torn to pieces. Some twenty minutes after my furnace fires had been extinguished, and when the ship was on the point of settling, every man, in obedience to a previous order which had been given the crew, jumped overboard, and endeavoured to save himself. There was no appearance of any boat coming to me from the enemy, until after my ship went down."

All would have drowned, for the *Kearsarge's* boats were disabled, and there was much delay in getting two afloat, and then not until ten men had perished. Fortunately, an English steam yacht, the *Deerhound,* owned by a gentleman named Lancaster, and two French fishing vessels hastened to the scene. In this way Captain Semmes and many of his officers and men were rescued.

The battle over, the victor, her crew almost unscathed, steamed away with flying colours to revel in the plaudits of their countrymen, and the Paris and London newspapers chronicled next day "La Mort de l'*Alamaba*," and "End of the famous *Alabama*."

But there was one little scene on the quay at Cherbourg when a small body of haggard, weather-beaten men—with their wounds still bleeding—were helped ashore, that deserves to be recorded. A thousand cheering French men and women and a few English and Americans rushed forward to greet them, to offer them small gifts and refreshment and to embrace them to applaud their heroism. Young Dayton thought this an "indecent spectacle" on the part of the Cherbourg population towards "pirates" and "rebels"; but pirates and rebels have always touched a more vibrant chord in the popular heart than even saints and mediocrities, while sympathy for the gallant vanquished is a humane emotion. "After all," as one Confederate sailor told a Paris reporter, "we have only been fighting for our country: not for ourselves. I have been two years afloat, I have a wife and two children in Mobile, and now I haven't a *sou* in the world."

"The loss of the *Alabama*," wrote Secretary Mallory to Bulloch, when the news reached Richmond (July 8):

"was announced in the Federal papers with all the manifestations of joy, which usually usher the news of great national victories, showing that the calculating enemy fully understood and appreciated the importance of her destruction. You must supply her place if possible, a measure which, important in itself, the information conveyed by your letter renders of paramount importance."

It is pleasant to be able to add that several of the French mariners who went to the rescue of the *Alabama's* drowning crew, one pilot named Mauger having saved twelve men, were granted gold and silver medals by the Emperor and cited in the *Moniteur*. For saving others of the crew, including the captain and several officers, the English yachtsman, Lancaster, was held up to opprobrium by some of the Federal newspapers, and the pleasant dictum of Secretary Seward, "It was the *right* of the *Kearsarge* that the pirates should drown," was widely approved in the North, though it rather shocked Lord Russell.

BUT Death, which "loves a shining mark," this year in France was lurking in the offing ready to pounce upon other than Confederate ships and sailors.

One evening—it was the first of December, 1864— as the American Minister, William Dayton, was rising from dinner, a servant handed him a letter which had just been left with the concierge. He opened it and read:

"SIR:

"This is to inform you that your Secretary of Legation, Mr. Pennington, is jeopardising your prestige and the honour of the United States by his scandalous liaison with the former Sophie Bricard, now known as Mrs. Eccles, and a rebel spy. The writer knows for a fact that Pennington will be spending this evening alone with this *lady* at her apartment at the Louvre Hotel. This ought to be stopped. It is your duty, Sir, to stop it."

The letter was signed "An Outraged American."

The Minister was much perturbed. He was a quiet, old-fashioned person, in spite of his occasional mild gallantries and fondness for French wines and cookery. Both he and Mrs. Dayton had long remarked the excessive number of his secretary's nightly engagements, which, they hoped, were inspired by social and diplomatic zeal. So this was the explanation!

The Minister was aware that for some time the most respectable Southerners in Paris had hesitated to set foot in the apartment of the lady who called herself Mrs. Eccles, or even to recognise her in public. Official people such as the Slidells, the Bullochs, the

Buchanans, the Huses and other Confederate agents
and emissaries gave her a wide berth. He vaguely remembered hearing that this was because of a warning
issued by Secretary Benjamin that the lady's be-
haviour and manner of life were the subject of much
complaint and reflected no credit on the Secessionist
cause.

It was clearly inadmissible that such a lady should
have relations with his secretary. Righteously indignant, the Minister resolved to take instant action. His
son William was just leaving for the theatre; he said
he would accompany him, as he had a call to make
in the locality.

They entered the carriage together and were driven
rapidly in the direction of the Louvre. There father
and son parted. At the hotel indicated Dayton enquired of the concierge the situation of Mrs. Eccles's
apartment. It was on the third floor; the staircase was
steep, and when a coloured manservant opened the
door he noticed that the elderly visitor was panting
for breath.

"Monsieur Pennington—*est-il ici?*" were his first
words.

Taken aback, the servant stammeringly requested
the visitor's name.

"It's of no consequence," was the reply. "Just say

that a gentleman would like to speak to him for a moment."

He heard sounds of a woman singing; this stopped suddenly, the door was flung open and the lady he remembered as Mademoiselle Bricard herself emerged. At the sight of the American Minister, she paused in great surprise. Recovering herself, she smilingly bade him enter. The Minister, still breathing heavily, asked again, "Is Mr. Pennington here?"

She replied, "To what, Mr. Dayton, do I owe the honour of this visit?"

"Perhaps you will kindly answer me, madam. If my secretary is under your roof, I should like to speak a moment with him."

"Mr. Pennington is not here."

The Minister was embarrassed. "I beg your pardon. I was informed—" he began huskily, and then stopped. His body swayed perilously to and fro; he seemed about to fall. In considerable alarm both the lady and her servant sprang forward to support him. They led him into the salon and assisted him to be seated.

"I apologise, madam," murmured Dayton, as soon as he could speak. "As you see, I am a little indisposed."

By this time the ci-devant Sophie Bricard had completely recovered her *aplomb*. She went to the buffet, took out a decanter of brandy and insisted on her distinguished though uninvited guest swallowing some of the liquor. This appeared to relieve him and he attempted to get on his feet. She restrained him gently, saying, "Wait a little. You will feel better presently. As for Mr. Pennington, I believe he is with a party at the theatre. If your business is very urgent, I could send for him."

"You are very kind, but do not trouble. At least, you admit that Mr. Pennington frequents your house —that you and he are on intimate terms." She did not deny this and he went on slowly, "Of course, madam, you are fully aware of the compromising character of this relationship—that if it were publicly known it would cost him his future career and seriously, perhaps irreparably, damage my own?"

The lady smiled. "Your Excellency is very frank. On what grounds do you question your secretary's right to my acquaintance—moral or political?" The Minister flushed.

"You are avowedly, madam, an enemy of the United States."

"I can convince you, Mr. Dayton, that you are quite mistaken. Have you seen Mr. Consul-General Bigelow lately?"

"I saw him yesterday."

"It is strange that he has never informed you that I have recently rendered him a service for which he is grateful. As a matter of fact, Mr. Dayton, for more than a year past I have ceased to interest myself in the Southern cause."

Her visitor expressed his surprise, and the lady went on, "I believe, Mr. Dayton, that you have never spoken against me, except that you thought I was 'misguided.' Well, it is true—I was. I expected better treatment from my own people. In giving me a bad name the Yankees in Paris fancied they were only doing their duty, I suppose. But these others—these *Southerners*—for these chivalrous gentlemen who I thought would back me up and be grateful to me for all I tried to do for the Cause right from the beginning, I have now only contempt. They threw me over, utter sycophants and hypocrites that they are! because, being an artist as well as a woman, I didn't conform to their narrow social code. Would you believe that the Jew, Benjamin, wrote to tell Mr. Slidell and the rest to 'wash their hands of me'! Oh, I know exactly what he wrote, for I have a copy of his letter. He called me a 'young woman of dubious morals, whose championship would compromise the Cause.' This, after all I did for the South here! You know it was I who first won over the Emperor and so made many things possible for Slidell? It was I who introduced many useful people to him and to Captain Bulloch. I gave up my career, I flung myself into the Cause, and what did I get for my pains? I was not *respectable* enough for them, and they gave me the cold shoulder. Can you wonder if I got sick of it all? I, who had sacrificed my art, my health, my peace of mind!"

She spoke with intense animation and bitterness. Dayton was highly astonished at her avowal. He perceived that she was suffering from wounded vanity. But he was still on his guard. Personally, he found her a strangely attractive young woman, though he suspected her to be unscrupulous. It was quite possible that the whole of this scene might be only a clever woman's stratagem to entrap him.

Then she opened a drawer and took out several letters bearing the address and seal of the United States Consulate, proving that she was really, as she alleged, in the secret service of his country.

"One thing more, Mr. Dayton. You come here expecting to find Mr. Pennington. He is a friend of mine and takes his diplomatic career seriously. I have often been useful to him, but he has probably not thought it prudent to mention it to you. As for my moral character, sir, I leave that to my enemies. I will only remind you that I am an American lady, here in Paris, without husband or other relative to protect me from slander.

"If I am at times unconventional, I owe no one any apology for my conduct." *

All this was delivered with such dignity that the Minister, gazing at her attentively, began to feel that he had done her a great injustice.

"What you tell me puts a different aspect on the matter," he said.

The events of the next ten minutes are obscure. According to the servant's account, the Minister's departure was delayed on one pretext or another. He and his hostess embarked on a friendly conversation. A bottle of champagne was introduced. From time to time Mr. Dayton placed his hand, and once both hands, on his temples, as if in pain or perplexity. At last he said,

"Your friends must regret that you abandoned the stage, madam. I remember your voice with pleasure,

---

* The reader should be warned that the whole of this high-flown dialogue is taken from a sensational brochure, *The True Account of the Death of Minister Dayton,* formerly in the possession of Judge Walter Berry. It was certified by the late Henry Vignaud as "exaggerated, but not improbable." It is clearly inspired if not actually written by the lady herself.

although it was then raised against us. Do you still sing?"

"She rose, laughingly, and went to the piano. She chose an aria out of *Florian* in which she had made her début three years before—the début at which Dayton had been present. Towards the close she heard a groan and a dull thud on the floor. She turned and, to her horror, saw that the Minister had fallen out of his chair and now lay rolling on the carpet in a sort of paroxysm. She knelt beside him: his eyeballs protruded, his lips were twisted in a hideous grimace. Her shrieks were answered by the negro servant. Water was poured over Dayton's features, his temples and hands were chafed; but all in vain. Mrs. E—— bade the servant go and summon the concierge and then run for a doctor. A key turned in the lock and P—— entered. Taking in the scene at a glance, he cried,

" 'Good God! What has happened? Who is this man?'

"He hastened forward, recognising Mr. Dayton, and felt his heart: it was motionless. Sophie explained breathlessly what had happened."

The nature of the predicament in which he was placed must now have struck Pennington. Nobody would understand the peculiar circumstances. A huge public scandal was certain if it was known that the

W. L. Dayton
American Minister to France, 1861-4

United States Minister had been found dead in the apartment of the former Sophie Bricard, whom an Abolitionist tourist had once described as "a shameless Jezebel of Secession." One thing was imperative—the body must be taken to the Legation. But was it not too late?

Descending the stairs he collided with the manager of the hotel, to whom Pennington swiftly explained his intentions. Removing a dead body from a house in France without notifying the police was a serious offence, but it had to be done. The doctor arrived. Sophie assisting him, they propped the corpse in a chair and fastened a neckerchief about the eyes. Then, together with the negro servant (half out of her wits with fright), they carried the Minister downstairs. It was no easy task, for Dayton was of heavy build, but they somehow managed it. The manager returned with a *fiacre*. Happily the driver proved a muscular fellow, who, when it was explained that the gentleman had had a fit, seized the body of Dayton under the armpits and deposited him more or less gently in a reclining posture inside the vehicle. Then, to Pennington's dismay, Mrs. Eccles appeared in wrap and bonnet, insisting on accompanying the body and explaining the whole affair to Mrs. Dayton. But this Pennington absolutely refused. While he was giving instructions to the driver the corpse nearly toppled forward, the doctor having relaxed his hold.

"*Dépêchez-vous!*" cried Pennington to the cabman. But the latter seemed in no hurry to ascend to his box.

"*Voyons!*" he said surlily, "I don't altogether like the look of this." And then, with a jerk of his thumb, "*Ce gaillard-là, il est mort pour sûr.*"

"Imbecile! Can't you see he is only ill? Drive on!" shouted Pennington, pushing a napoleon into the man's palm. "Drive as fast as you can to the doctor's, 25 Rue Circulaire." The fellow grunted and climbed to his seat. A gendarme was already crossing the square in their direction with enquiry written plainly on his features; but in another moment the driver was lashing his horse. The midnight journey up the Champs-Elysées with the body of the American Minister had begun.

Next day, the newspapers announced with the usual conventional expressions of regret that his Excellency, William L. Dayton, Envoy Extraordinary and Minister Plenipotentiary of the United States in Paris, had passed away suddenly at the Legation as the result of an apoplectic stroke.

CHAPTER X

ESCAPE OF THE "STONEWALL"

BY the autumn of 1864 all Slidell's protracted efforts to come to terms with the French Government as regards the ships approaching completion at Bordeaux and Nantes had ended in utter failure. The vessels had been sold, Arman and Voruz had got their money and to both Slidell and Bulloch's extreme mortification Prussian and Danish naval officers were walking the decks and supervising the finishing touches to their newly-acquired property.

But even now not all hope was abandoned. The Prussian-Danish war might come to a sudden end, and the protagonists consent to dispose of one or more of the ships. Indeed, an armistice did occur and two of the corvettes and a ram were hurried off to Prussia. The remaining ram now became the single object of Bulloch's attention. There was just a chance of reclaiming her. He did not dare to go himself to Bordeaux; to be seen there would have excited instant suspicion. He cast about for a cool and competent spy and his choice fell upon Captain Emile Tessier, a New Orleans man who had commanded a Mississippi steamboat in his time and had seen much and varied service afloat. With Arman's connivance Tessier wandered about the shipyard and scrutinised the ram at close quarters. He reported to Bulloch that the Danish engineer was making certain alterations and adopting another method of riveting the armour-plates which he was sure Bulloch would not approve. But although the war about Schleswig-Holstein was over before the ram could be launched, there was no sign that the Danish Minister of Marine would like to get out of his bargain. Tessier's report was that the Danish engineers were satisfied and when therefore Bulloch learned that the ram had actually sailed for Copenhagen he decided, at last, though reluctantly, to wash his hands of the whole affair.

> "I had every reason [he explains] to suppose that the sale to Denmark was to be *bona fide,* both by the French Foreign Office and the United States Minister, and I thought it would be imprudent to enter into an engagement which could by any possibility arouse suspicion and again draw attention to a Confederate agent."

At this juncture, November, 1864, a new and picturesque figure appears on the scene, a French soldier of fortune, calling himself the Baron Henri Arnous de Rivière. This personage, whom Major Huse came to describe as "one of the most accomplished and unscrupulous men I have ever met," had in the course of twenty years showed his scarred and tanned face in half the seaports of the world. A former French officer of engineers, he had lived in India, China, Mexico and Peru. He had been a mining prospector in Bolivia and was said still to own a mine there; he had also served in the Chilean army. Arman had known him for years. When De Rivière heard about the ram built for the Confederacy which Arman was being forced to deliver to Denmark, his interest was instantly aroused.

"I will go with you to Copenhagen," he exclaimed. "My sympathies are ardently for the Confederates. Perhaps we may find a way of getting the ship back from the Danes." This proposal, when it was transmitted by Arman to Bulloch, fell on stony ground. Bulloch persisted in his resolve to have nothing further to do with the affair.

Some weeks elapsed; a caller presented himself at Captain Bulloch's hotel in Liverpool. It was the Baron Arnous de Rivière.

"Captain Bulloch," he announced, "I am just back from Copenhagen and have the honour to inform you that the Arman ram there is now at the disposal of your Government."

De Rivière proceeded to relate an extraordinary and indeed outrageous story.

He had gone with M. Arman to Copenhagen. The ship en route to the Danish port had been subjected to a trial. This trial would have been perfectly satisfactory to the Danish naval authorities if De Rivière himself had not resorted to a daring stratagem. Inviting the party of Danes to lunch on board, he had excused himself, gone below and opened a bilgecock, partially filling one of the compartments and so reducing the speed of the vessel. A full head of steam was on at the time and yet, strange to say, not even the captain and engineer of the *Stoerkodder* (as the ram was now called) suspected what had happened.

After lunch the party came on deck and were astonished to find the ship running so badly. The Danish engineers shook their heads and decided that the vessel had not come up to specification. Arman naturally protested, until De Rivière took him aside and said, "Don't say a word. It's all right. They'll give her up now. Leave it to me."

So the report officially condemned the *Stoerkodder:*

the bargain with Arman was repudiated and the vessel now only awaited a change of captain and crew to fulfil her original destiny.

All this was rather too lawless for Bulloch. It offended his sense of professional decency. He immediately conceived a deepening dislike and distrust of this audacious Frenchman. He adhered therefore to his former resolution.

"This game you propose is a bit too risky for me, Baron," he said. "You'll have to find some one else."

"What!" cried the other. "You refuse?"

"Absolutely."

"Very well, Sir. There are other men in the Confederate service who will not hesitate to seize this splendid chance."

De Rivière forthwith hurried off to broach the scheme to Major Caleb Huse, the Confederate military agent, with whom he had a slight acquaintance. Huse now lived in Paris, but made occasional visits to London. In Jermyn Street de Rivière was told that Huse had just gone to his bank in the City. Hailing a hansom cab, the Baron drove off instantly to Bishopsgate Street. On the pavement outside the bank he recognised the Major and called to him by name, asking him to get into the cab.

"I did so," testified Huse in a letter written many
years afterwards to Bigelow, "and was immediately
asked if I 'would like to do something worth while.'
I replied, 'What is it?' and then de Rivière said that
the ram which had been taken to Copenhagen was
still there, that he had conceived and partially carried out a plan of getting her into the hands of the
Confederates, but that Bulloch would not co-operate
with him. Would I?

"I replied that I was no sailor, and did not see how
I could undertake what so clever a man as Bulloch
thought impracticable—for he was a man of great
ability, and I did not see what I could do.... De
Rivière said, 'Now, there is the ship. She has on
board guns capable of piercing anything the United
States has at sea and her armour is invulnerable
against any gun they have afloat." '

It was certainly a tempting proposal for a warrior
of spirit who had been so long condemned to military
inaction.

In the end Huse was so impressed that he agreed to
accompany de Rivière to Paris and consult Slidell.
They took the night boat and the next morning Huse
went to the Avenue d'Antin and told Slidell the whole
story.

But Bulloch had already written and explained the
motive of his refusal. In Huse's opinion Bulloch was

"afraid to deal with so unmitigated a scoundrel as he believed de Rivière to be."

Slidell thought the attempt ought certainly to be made. Whereupon Huse went to his house in Auteuil and informed his wife of the whole affair, saying that if she as well as Slidell offered no objection, he proposed to embark upon the adventure.

Mrs. Huse broke into peals of laughter.

"Why, Caleb," she cried, "you are no sailor! You know nothing whatever about a ship and you are always seasick."

Seeing, however, that her husband was in grim earnest, she added, after a moment's reflection:

"You have had no chance in this war and I can see that here is an opportunity to gain no little credit. I should be willing to have you go if one man were here to go with you. He is a sailor and is devoted to you."

The man she referred to was Major John Pierson, Huse's bosom friend and trusted associate in shipping arms from Europe to the Confederacy.

"That," replied her husband, "is impossible. Pierson is in Texas."

"We sat down to breakfast," relates Huse. "It was then about eleven o'clock. In a few minutes we were astounded to have Pierson enter the room. He had

just arrived from Texas, by way of Havana. I told
him the story and he at once consented to accompany me.

"We went at once to Mr. Slidell's and from there
to Erlanger's, where I arranged for £1,000 in gold
to be ready for me that evening at the Northern
Railway station."

Slidell furnished Huse with the necessary written
authority to take command of the ship when de Rivière, acting as Arman's agent, had got re-possession of
it from the Danish authorities. De Rivière himself had
gone on to Copenhagen in advance, and both Slidell
and Huse entertained a fear that he might actually
attempt to get together a crew and sail the ship out on
his own account!

At the appointed hour Huse and Pierson met at the
Gare du Nord in Paris.

"We started, carrying our bag of gold ourselves,
and I never realised before how heavy gold is; a
man would soon tire of carrying all the time even a
small salary in gold.

With this passing commentary, which perhaps ex-
plains the universal popularity of a valid but impon-
derable paper currency, Huse is silent about his journey to Copenhagen, where they were met by both De
Rivière and Arman. Huse continues:

"My plan was simply to sail the ship to Charleston or Wilmington and I have no doubt one or two things would have happened, either we should have gone to the bottom or got there.... I must have arrived, if at all, in time for at least the *time* of the ending of the war to be delayed and possibly the final result would have been different. There is no denying that the *Stonewall* * was a very formidable ship, and it is safe to say that her arrival in a Confederate States port would have given new life to the South and it is hardly too much to believe that under a skilful commander she would have opened the principal ports at once and even had things her own way in offensive operations.

"Had the *Stonewall* arrived at all under my command she would have been on the coast *at least* two months before she did arrive at Havana; indeed I believe she would have appeared on the coast by the middle of February."

But at Copenhagen, to Huse's intense surprise and, one can well believe, his chagrin, he encountered next day a third man. That man was Bulloch himself. He had suddenly changed his mind and hurried northward. In his *Memoirs* Bulloch gives as a reason his discovery that the circumstances had changed. The vessel was clear of French interference. She was in

* As the *Stoerkodden* was soon afterwards re-christened.

Copenhagen and the purchasers were now anxious to annul their bargain.

Arman, proving that he was a real friend of the Confederacy, proposed to instruct his agent, de Rivière, to manage the negotiations with the Danish authorities so as to give Bulloch time to collect a staff of officers, prepare the necessary supply of stores and a tender, and select a suitable rendezvous. Bulloch records:

> "He [Arman] said that when I was ready his agent would get leave to engage a Danish crew to navigate the ship back to Bordeaux, but instead of returning to that port he would take her to the appointed rendezvous, and deliver her to the Confederate officer appointed to command her."

Bulloch sent for Tessier and Captain Thomas F. Page to join him at Copenhagen. In all this there was no rôle allotted to Huse and Pierson: so they reluctantly returned to Paris; the great scheme had been entrusted to other hands. Perhaps Mrs. Huse breathed a sigh of relief. Huse says:

> "My action in the matter offended Bulloch intensely. We had been warm friends. I saw him but once or twice afterwards, on one of which occasions he simply—and very rightly—said, 'Well, you might have had confidence enough in me to have told me what you intended doing. Your success would have

been my disgrace. I deserved better treatment at your hands.' All of which was true and he was justly offended.

"But what was to be done must be done quickly, and I had been my own master so completely for the whole war and had succeeded so completely in everything I had undertaken, that I came insensibly to run everything by my own will, taking counsel of nobody." *

Whether or not Huse would have succeeded, it turned out that Bulloch's choice of Captain Page to command the enterprise was not altogether happy. Although "an old and experienced officer, bred in the United States navy and sent out from Richmond to command one of the so-called Birkenhead rams," Page sadly lacked initiative and audacity. "He had kept himself so completely out of sight since his arrival in Europe that it was felt to be almost certain that he would not be known to any spy whom the United States officials might employ to watch the ship; besides which, he was a man particularly well-suited for secret service by reason of a marked constitutional tendency to silence and reserve when among strangers or newly-made acquaintances."

Page now found himself summoned from Paris to

* The whole of Huse's letter is printed in Bigelow's *Retrospections of a Long Life.*

Copenhagen to make a clandestine acquaintance with the *Stoerkodder* as long as she remained nominally in Danish hands. He was enjoined to keep in constant touch with Arman's agents, and take passage in the ship for the rendezvous, which was to be off the French coast at Ile d'Houat, opposite Quiberon Bay. There she would receive her arms and change her crew for a Confederate complement.

But the arrangement for this transfer proved a very complicated and delicate proceeding. It involved the purchase or hire by Bulloch of a steam tender in England, to carry the ordnance and crew alongside the *Stoerkodder*. The Confederate exchequer in Europe was very low just then, but luckily Bulloch got hold of the owner of an old blockade-runner who put his vessel at his service. Choosing the officers and crew was comparatively easy. Paris just then was full of men who had been discharged from the *Florida* and *Rappahannock,* but getting them away to an English port or into English waters was an exciting and dangerous business, for the ports were full of spies, on the watch for the slightest breach of neutrality. It also took time, when time was so precious.

At Copenhagen also de Rivière was having trouble with his Danish crew, a number of whom, getting wind of the plot in which they were engaged, refused to serve. The others had to be bribed and bullied; but at last, with a young and very inexperienced engineer, the *Stoerkodder* steamed out of Copenhagen harbour on the 6th of January, 1865, ostensibly bound for Bordeaux.

A few days later the officers and crew assembled at Calais, crossed the Channel, and joined the blockade-runner which was lying in the Thames. All this time the United States ship *Niagara* was on the watch at Dover, but they managed to give her the slip. A terrific tempest arose and the heavily-laden tender was forced to seek shelter under Cherbourg breakwater.

On the 13th Lieutenant Davidson, in command of the tender, reported:

> "It was indeed lucky that I determined to come down Channel on the French coast, for the steamer would have suffered on the English side from the heavy sea, besides which, I might have been forced into one of the harbours on that side. Your officers and men are all very manageable, and we get on very well. The chances are now that this part of the expedition is all right."

The wintry storm continued and the tender could not get away before the 18th.

Meanwhile Captain Page, on board the liberated ironclad, had stopped to coal at Niewe Diep in Holland and not until the 24th did they get to Quiberon Bay, where the tender had been waiting four days. At the Island of Houat the transfer of crews was made and the *Stoerkodder,* with a hundred and twenty-five Southern sailors aboard, became at last the Confederate States' warship, *Stonewall,* named in honour of the famous general, and so set forth on her voyage of expected triumph and destruction.*

In Paris the secret was out. Bigelow, now American Chargé d'Affaires, who thought he had forever frustrated Arman's schemes, was in full hue and cry. On the 28th January, the moment the news reached him, he wrote to Drouyn de Lhuys:

> "I am advised of an ironclad vessel recently built at Bordeaux, arriving under the Danish flag, with a Danish captain and crew on board, at the Isle of Houat. She has discharged her Danish crew, who were taken to Quiberon in a vessel sent to supply her with coals by Messrs. Dubigeon fils of St. Nazaire.

---

* The number of Federal vessels destroyed by Confederate Cruisers fitted out in England and France was as follows:

Ships	75	Steamers	3
Schooners	63	Gunboat	1
Barques	71	Pilot boats	2
Brigs	33	Cutter	1
Total value			$8,639,999.82

Cf. J. T. Scharf: *A History of the Confederate States Navy,* 1887.

"While taking in her coals an English steamer came alongside and supplied her with guns, munitions of war and a crew.

"Your Excellency, I trust, will not think I am too hasty in concluding that this vessel also is designed to prey upon American commerce under the flag of the so-called Confederate Government.

"I hasten to bring these facts to your Excellency's attention in the hopes that measures may be immediately taken to prevent a violation of that neutrality which the Imperial Government has shown itself so justly solicitous to maintain."

Although the next day was Sunday, Bigelow hastened to the Ministry of Marine and informed M. Chasseloup-Loubat, who professed entire ignorance of the matter, but said he would send off telegrams at once. Arman, he said, had deceived him twice and might try to do so again; if so, they could not help it, as the point where the vessels lay was not under guns of the Government. Bigelow protested that the transfer had occurred in French waters, that the vessel had been coaled clandestinely from a French steamer, and that intelligence of these facts had reached him indirectly through a French Government officer. The Minister repeated that the waters in which this vessel was lying were not under government surveillance; then (reported Bigelow to his government), "as if beginning to realise the weakness of that position, he took the ground that the vessel had been sold to the Danish Government, which had thereby become responsible for the use that should be made of it."

Bigelow asked if he had any evidence that the Danish Government had accepted the vessel before she left France. He replied that, as it was a vessel of war, it could not have received his authorisation to leave without first exhibiting a contract for its purchase by some neutral government; that her commander did produce one from the Danish Government, and if that Government did not intend to keep the ship, it should, by a proper notification, have placed it once more under French jurisdiction; till then, Denmark and not France was responsible for the vessel.

> "I betook myself immediately to the Danish Legation," states Bigelow, "but as Count Molkte, the Danish Minister in Paris, chanced to be absent, I called the following day, January 31, 1865, when I learned from him that there had been negotiations pending between his Government and Arman; but the Danish inspector had informed Arman before the vessel left Bordeaux that she would not be accepted, as she had not been delivered according to the conditions of the contract. Count Molkte said further, that Arman sent her to Copenhagen in spite

of this notice, with a French crew in charge of a M. Arnous de la Rivière; that on her arrival the crew was sent home, after lying there some three months; the Danish Government persisting in its refusal to accept her, Arnous hired a Danish captain and crew to bring the ship to Bordeaux. Count Molkte also informed me that Arnous had been to see him the day before in company with the Danish pilot and captain, and he gave as his reasons for stopping in the bay of Quiberon that his engineers were unskilful, his sailors mutinous, and his oil had given out. This last embarrassment struck the Count as quite a novelty in the category of maritime disasters, and helped to confirm his suspicions in regard to the whole transaction."

In speaking of the alleged defective construction of the *Stoerkodder,* Arnous admitted to Count Molkte her predatory destination. "She was a terrible vessel," he had boasted, "and was going to make terrible havoc among the blockading squadrons of the Federals."

It adds something to the piquancy of the situation to know that all this time Slidell was receiving the congratulations of his French friends, including more than one member of the Government, upon the successful escape of the *Stonewall* and hopes of her safe arrival in American waters. In the archives of the Ministry of Marine is the draft of a letter from the Marquis de Chasseloup-Loubat informing Slidell of Bigelow's indignant representations and the line which he proposed to take up with that gentleman, which reveals a private sportsmanlike satisfaction over the clever "getaway," a satisfaction which was probably shared by more than one occupant of the Tuileries.

Within a week all Paris was talking of the *Stonewall* and wagers were laid on the chances of her reaching her destination and getting into action. For by this time it was only too manifest that the Confederacy, hard-pressed by land and sea, was in a very bad way. The Northern forces had the port of Savannah in their grip, Charleston was almost beleaguered by land, as well as by sea, and Wilmington was threatened by a combined attack.

Thus, the South was becoming hermetically sealed, its Government was shut up in Richmond and Lee's army was holding Grant's forces at bay only by amazing strategy and heroism.

The arrival of the *Stonewall* might alter the whole situation. The hopes of the Confederacy may be said without exaggeration to have centred in that ironclad hull and eager crew.

A few days later and Slidell had a message from Bulloch at Dover that the U. S. S. *Niagara* had set off in pursuit; the next news was that the *Stonewall* had put into Ferrol in Spain, believed to have sprung a leak.

Owing to the crowded state of the ship, a satisfactory examination could not be made at sea; so Captain Page now first went into Corunna and then across the bay into Ferrol "where all facilities were tendered by the officers of the Naval Arsenal." Work was at once begun, but on the 7th Page wrote:

> "Today there came off an officer to inform me that in consequence of the protest of the American Minister the permission to repair damages had been suspended and I must restore the things in the hull to the ship."

Page added, however, that the officer commanding the arsenal told him that his case was under consideration at Madrid, and that he thought "all would be right in a few days." In the end permission was given to make all necessary repairs, but many difficulties were met with, the authorities appearing to be very desirous to hurry the ship off, while yet not willing to turn her out of port in an incomplete state.

On February 10th the U. S. S. *Niagara,* Captain Thomas Craven, steamed into Ferrol harbour, followed by the *Sacramento.* There they anchored, obviously watching the *Stonewall* closely and prepared to attack her whenever she was ready to leave. The *Stonewall's* repairs would, in Captain Page's opinion, require several weeks. It was all most unfortunate. Page, in view of the last news from America, was in doubt what to do. Finally, he decided to go to Paris and take Slidell's and Bulloch's advice.

By this time Slidell was deeply disappointed and filled with distrust of Page. He regretted that Bulloch had not allowed Huse to control the undertaking or had not taken the command himself.

> "I think," he told Page, "you take too gloomy a view of our military situation and that no immediate catastrophe is impending. It is too bad that having at length got this ship into our hands in November so much valuable time has been lost."

It was decided not to abandon the effort to reach the scene of war. Page was instructed to return to Ferrol, elude the enemy, sail to Bermuda, ship some more ordnance and crew, and then strike a blow at Port Royal, which was General Sherman's base in the Carolinas.

Page, therefore, rejoined his ship at Ferrol after more than six weeks' delay, expecting to find himself attacked by the two United States warships still on the *qui vive* in harbour.

But if Page was dilatory and unenterprising, his Federal naval antagonist, Craven, proved to be even more so. On March 24, the *Stonewall* steamed out of harbour. To Captain Page's astonishment the *Niagara* and *Sacramento* did not follow.

> "This," reported Page, "will doubtless seem as inexplicable to you as it is to me and to all of us. To suppose that those two heavily-armed men-of-war were *afraid* of the *Stonewall* is to me incredible. Yet the fact of their conduct was such as I have stated to you. Finding that they declined coming out, there was no course but for me to pursue my voyage."

Yet, incredible or not, the ironclad prow of the Southern ram was enough to fill the Northern commander with misgiving. The prospect of having his ships sent to the bottom of Corunna Bay at the very end of the war was too much for Craven. He would have to face the charge of cowardice, but better that than death and destruction. So the *Stonewall* steamed southward out of Ferrol with flying colours, escorted by a large Spanish frigate to the end of the three-mile limit, her crew hardly able to credit their extraordinary release.

Even now a bold, swift dash across the Atlantic might have borne fruit. But Page incomprehensibly dawdled. He coaled at Lisbon, hung about Teneriffe, and only got to Nassau six weeks later, on May 6th.

The War of Secession was over; the high hopes of officers and crew were utterly foiled and one hundred and twenty-five dejected men stepped finally ashore at Havana. The *Stonewall* was transferred to the Cuban authorities for a paltry $16,000, just enough to pay off the disconsolate crew.

There were many others who were equally dejected at the failure of the ultimate naval adventure of the Confederacy. In Paris, Slidell was divided between disappointment and anger at what he conceived to be Captain Page's mishandling of the whole enterprise. Bulloch was overwhelmed with regret, and avoided the reproaches of Colonel Huse. The Baron Arnous de Rivière was eloquent in his disgust.

Yet perhaps none felt the failure more than Arman, the builder of the *Stonewall*. From beginning to end he had suffered much humiliation and anxiety for his zeal in the Confederate cause; out of the six vessels he had built only one had escaped the clutches of international law. When after long intrigue and vicissitudes he had himself seen her safely piloted out of Copenhagen harbour and had heard from his friend, the Minister of Marine, Chasseloup-Loubat, that she had triumphantly passed through the twin ordeals of

Quiberon and Ferrol he was convinced that the moment of triumph was at hand.

We do not know what the French Emperor felt about the *Stonewall*. But we are not left without some evidence of his interest. In the year 1892 there was sold at the Hotel Drouot, Paris, the model of an ironclad ship of war, thirty-nine centimetres long, mounted on an ebony base and enclosed within a glass dome. There was a miniature ensign, with the letters, "C.S.A." and the proportions were exactly those of the lamented *Stonewall*. A label was attached in which the model was described as "formerly belonging to H. M. Napoleon III and removed with other objects from the Tuileries in 1871."

CHAPTER XI

THE END OF A PASSAGE

I firmly believe that if, after the reports of its Commissioners in Europe and the evidence of public reprehension in England and France, the Confederate junta in Richmond had thrown over slavery and had announced emancipation by purchase both the French and English governments would have recognised the Southern Confederacy and she would have taken her place amongst the nations of the earth.

—L. Q. C. Lamar

ONE of the most striking instances of political perversity in the history of nations—is the continued adhesion during four years of Jefferson Davis and the rulers of the Confederate States to the institution of slavery. To Slidell it was especially tragic because he, unlike his colleague Mason in England, really did not care a straw about slavery. When he came to see what a handicap it was to official recognition he would have promptly discarded it as a simple measure of self-preservation. But he was convinced that from the moment he should indicate his views to the Cabinet at Richmond, his recall would be cer-

tain. Thus, he remained silent on the subject, not only
to the French, but to his own Government. He knew
that De Leon had been sent over specially charged
to report upon his personal opinions and his diplomatic conduct. He was likewise aware that the egre-
gious Dudley Mann was ready to supersede him in
Paris. So the only possible course was to remain quiet
and hope for a decisive victory for Southern arms.

It is not as if President Davis and his advisers were
ignorant of the state of French public opinion.

"It has been impossible," wrote Benjamin (January
9, 1864) to one of his emissaries, Henry Hotze, then
in France, "to remain blind to the evidence of the
articles which emanate from the best known names
in French literature. In what is perhaps the most
powerful and influential of the French periodicals,
La Revue des Deux-Mondes, there is scarcely any
article signed by the members of its able corps of
contributors which does not contain some disparag-
ing allusion to the South. Abolition sentiments are
quietly assumed as philosophical axioms too self-
evident to require comment or elaboration, and the
result of this struggle is in all cases treated as a fore-
gone conclusion, and nothing is within the range of
possibility except the subjugation of the South and
the emancipation of the whole body of the negroes.
The example of San Domingo does not seem in the

least to disturb the faith of these philanthropists in the entire justice and policy of a war waged for this end, and our resistance to the fate proposed for us is treated as a crime against liberty and civilisation. The Emperor is believed by us to be sincerely desirous of putting an end to the war by the recognition of our independence; but powerful as he is, he is too sagacious to act in direct contravention of the settled public opinion of his people, while hampered by the opposition of the English Government."

After reading this one marvels all the more at the political inflexibility which so fatuously resisted every friendly counsel in a matter admittedly vital to the success of the cause.

"Slavery," De Leon had reported some months before, "is the real bête noir of the French imagination.... Almost incredible as it may appear, the Slavery Question is more of a stumbling-block to our recognition in France than in England for it is really and truly a matter of sentiment with the French people, who ever have been more swayed by such consideration than their cooler and more calculating neighbours on the other side of the channel.

"From the hour of my arrival here until today the same thing has been repeated over and over again by persons connected with the Government and enjoying the confidence of the Emperor, 'France cannot take the lead in acknowledging the Southern Con-

federacy without some promise for prospective
emancipation.'

"The same statement was made by one of our
warmest friends in the French Ministry, and one
nearest the Emperor—Count de Persigny, but three
days ago—and M. de Lesseps says the same. It is
vain to tell them how utterly impracticable such a
proposition must be and that the Southern People
never would consent to purchase recognition at the
price of such a concession of wrong-doing—as it
would imply; the answer is always the same: 'Well,
then, the feeling of our people compels us to make
the condition.'

"Against a rooted prejudice and a preconceived
opinion like this, reason and argument are powerless,
and the concessions demanded would deprive the
gift of all value if accorded, besides humiliating us to
the level desired by our enemies. Therefore it is that,
despairing of removing by diplomatic efforts the
calculating selfishness of England and the senti-
mental repugnance of France, I have counselled, and
now reiterate the suggestion, *the entire suppression
of the attempt made through accredited Commissioners in Europe for recognition, waiving the question of the heavy expenditure thereby incurred, and
placing the matter on the footing of self-respect and
true policy.* I may add also that in the opinion of influential and sagacious French statesmen such a step
would produce a most favourable impression on the

public sentiment here, which responds to such appeals."

This being written in Slidell's office in Paris and entirely without consulting him, his indignation when he learnt of it will appear natural.* He soon came to look upon De Leon as a spy and when he found him actually tampering with his letters protested so angrily to Richmond that De Leon was himself recalled.

Being first and foremost a lawyer, Benjamin's pronouncements upon slavery were in strict, even pedantic accordance with his brief. He, consulting his clients, refused to consider the subject from the point of view either of humanity or expediency. If he had been less the lawyer than the statesman, and still more the Southern patriot, he would have turned upon Jefferson Davis and the slavery intransigents and given them the straight, sound and wise counsel they needed. As it was, there was no man wilier in shifting the grounds of an argument to a severely legal and academic plane. This was conspicuously shown when

---

* Replying to De Leon (August 17, 1863), Benjamin wrote:
"In relation to your remarks about the withdrawal of our Commissioners from Europe, it is only necessary to say that there were other than diplomatic interests entrusted to them which could be known only to the Government and which rendered their presence abroad necessary to the public interests."

the unhappy Mason, after less than a year of English reproaches, both public and private, on the subject of slavery unbosomed himself to his Secretary of State. It appeared that he had been dining with Lord Donoughmore, a peer, an ex-President of the Board of Trade and a warm and earnest friend of the South. There was then talk of impending recognition and an Anglo-Confederate treaty. Did the Confederacy intend to continue the slave trade? If so, Lord Palmerston would never consent to any treaty.

"Such was the sentiment of England on this subject, that no Minister could hold his place for a day, who should negotiate a Treaty with any power not containing such a clause; nor could any House of Commons be found, which would sustain a Minister thus delinquent, *and he referred to the fact,* (as he alleged it to be,) *that in every existing Treaty with England that prohibition was contained.* He said further, that he did not mean to express his individual opinion, but that he was equally satisfied, should the Palmerston Ministry go out, and the Tories come in, such would likewise be their necessary policy; and he added that he was well assured that England and France would be in accord on that subject."

In reply, Mason told Lord Donoughmore that he feared this

"would form a formidable obstacle, if persisted in, to any Treaty; that he must be aware on all questions affecting African servitude, our government was naturally and necessarily sensitive, when presented by any foreign Power. We had learned from abundant experience that the Anti-slavery sentiment was always aggressive; that this condition of society was one with which, in our opinion, the destinies of the South were indissolubly connected; that as regarded foreign Powers, it was with us a question purely domestic, with which our safety required that none such should, in any manner, interfere."

Mason was persuaded he knew the views of his Government, but pleaded that he had been given no special instructions on the forbidden subject. Benjamin had no desire to compile any special instructions: but at last driven to defend categorically the policy of his Government, he therefore wrote (January 15, 1863) a portentous paper, beginning:

"It has been suggested to this Government, from a source of unquestioned authority, that after the recognition of our independence by the European powers, an expectation is generally entertained by them that in our treaties of amity and commerce a clause will be introduced making stipulations against the African slave-trade. It is even thought that neutral powers may be inclined to insist upon the insertion of such a clause as a *sine qua non*.

"After conference with the President, we have come to the conclusion that the best mode of meeting the question is to assume the constitutional ground."

With this prologue Benjamin proceeded at great and wearisome length to expound the Confederate constitutional position as regards the slave trade. According to the constitution, the States had reserved to themselves the right to deal with the slave traffic, and the treaty-making power, and that consequently the President and Senate were debarred from action.

"There is not only an absence of express delegation of authority to the treaty-making power, which alone would suffice to prevent the exercise of such authority, but there is the implied prohibition resulting from the fact that all duty on the subject is imposed on a different branch of the government.

"I need scarcely enlarge upon the familiar principle that authority expressly delegated to Congress cannot be assumed in our government by the treaty-making power. The authority to lay and collect taxes, to coin money, to declare war, etc., are ready examples, and you can be at no loss for argument or illustration in support of so well recognised a principle.

"It is thus seen that while the States were willing to trust Congress with the power to prohibit the introduction of African slaves from the United States, they were not willing to trust it with the power of prohibiting their introduction from any other quarter, but determined to insure the execution of their will by a direct interposition of their own power.

"Moreover, any attempt on the part of the treaty-making power of this government to prohibit the African slave-trade, in addition to the insuperable objection above suggested, would leave open the implication that the same power has authority to permit such introduction. No such implication can be sanctioned by us. This government unequivocally and absolutely denies its possession of any power whatever over the subject, and cannot entertain any proposition in relation to it."

But all this quibbling about constitutionality and legislative procedure was quite inexplicable to Europe. Nor was it any real answer to the question.

James Spence was an ardent pro-Confederate and had rendered such service to the cause both in England and France that he had been taken into the service as a paid propagandist. But Spence was no believer in slavery; and, moreover, as a sensible man he did not believe that sensible people in the South believed in it. So he wrote a pamphlet in which he repeated some very hard but very true things about slavery.

"In fact, slavery, like other wrongs, reacts on the wrong-doer. Taking the most temperate view of it, stripping away all exaggerations, it remains an evil in an economical sense, a wrong to humanity in a moral one. It is a gross anachronism, a thing of two thousand years ago; the brute force of dark ages obtruding into the midst of the nineteenth century; a remnant of elder dispensations whose harsh spirit was law, in conflict with the genius of Christianity, whose mild spirit is love. No reasoning, no statistics, no profit, no philosophy can reconcile us to that which our instinct repels. After all the arguments have been poured into the ear there is something in the heart that spurns them. We make no declaration that all men are born equal, but a conviction—innate, irresistible—tells us, with a voice we cannot stifle, that a man is a man, and not a chattel. Remove from slavery, as it is well to do, all romance and exaggeration, in order that we may deal with it wisely and calmly, it remains a foul blot, from which all must desire to purge the annals of the age."

Spence's direct appeal to Benjamin as "a man of the world" and in the true interests of the Confederacy to execute a healthy *volte face* on the slavery question brought the lawyer promptly down from his dialectics and cloudy evasions. He became a man of the world and a very practical politician and James Spence was dismissed from his post. Benjamin wrote:

"I feel some embarrassment in replying to your observations on the subject of slavery, but will be entirely frank in what I have to say. I freely admit that, as a private gentleman entirely disconnected from this government, you could not, consistently with self-respect, conceal or colour your true sentiments on this or any other question in which principles are involved. It is also quite probable that the fact of your entertaining the opinions which you profess renders your advocacy of our cause more effective with a people whose views coincide with yours, and it would be folly on our part to request the aid or alienate the feelings of those who, while friendly to our cause, are opposed to the institutions established among us. On the other hand, it appears to me that candour requires on your part the concession that no government could justify itself before the people whose servant it is, if it selected as exponents of its views and opinions those who entertain sentiments decidedly averse to an institution which both the government and the people maintain as essential to their wellbeing. The question of slavery is one in which all the most important interests of our people are involved, and they have the right to expect that their government, in the selection of the agents engaged in its service, should refuse to retain those who are in avowed and public opposition to their opinions and feelings. I answer your appeal, therefore, by saying that, 'as a man of the world,' I would meet you on the most cordial terms without the slightest reference to your views on this subject; but that, 'as a member of a government,' it would be impossible for me to engage you in its service after the publication of your opinions." *

No wonder that Bigelow afterwards came to speculate upon "the infatuation of those Richmond statesmen which approached dementia."

"They depended for the success of their revolt, as they confessed, upon the sympathy and co-operation of two powerful European States, in neither of which could be found a single statesman who would have dared to speak of slavery in any public assembly except in terms of abhorrence."

As an illustration of French anti-slavery sentiment, the following translation of an address signed by "Twelve French Patriots of Tours" in 1864 has a particular interest:

"To Monsieur Slidell, Commissioner of the Confederate States of America.
"Sir,
"We admit your countrymen are brave, that they are chivalrous to one another, loyal to their chiefs, capable of patriotic enthusiasm, of undergoing hardships, *but—do they support slavery?*

* Benjamin to Spence, January 11, 1864.

"We do not deny to the Southern people personal honour, magnanimity, self-respect, intelligence, *but* —do they keep their fellow-men in a degrading servitude because of their colour?

"We Frenchmen grant beauty, grace and chastity to your women, *but* before we render them our homage we ask: *Do they own slaves?*

"So far from denying your right to political freedom, to choose your own Government, to resist oppression, we approve and would aid you with all our power, *but* before we move one single inch we must insist on your reply to this question: Do you mean to uphold slavery—*do you still refuse freedom to the slaves?*

"Until you can answer this question, my dear Mr. Slidell, and answer it in one way, it is useless to make any appeal to the people of France. It may be our interest to support you: There may be strong material and political reasons for a close alliance between us, but as long as you maintain and are maintained by slavery we cannot offer you our alliance, but on the contrary, we hope and expect you will fail." *

At last the day dawned when even Jefferson Davis could no longer resist the logic or the necessities of the situation.

In the winter of 1864-65, the armed resistance of the

* Eustis papers.

South was fast growing enfeebled and the fabric of the Confederacy was crumbling. The same thing might even now save it, which could and would have saved it from the first, namely, recognition by either France or England, and the freedom of those ports where to the Confederacy might trade and carry their prizes.

Amongst the Southern Congressmen at Richmond there was one Duncan F. Kenner of Louisiana who had for some time offered conspicuous opposition to the bigoted majority. He was not only a slave-owner, but once told some of his fellow-members that he and his family probably owned more slaves than all of them put together. Kenner had long since been convinced that as long as the foundations of the Confederacy rested, or appeared to European eyes to rest, on the institution of slavery European recognition was impossible. He now urged upon President Davis the immediate despatch to England and France of a special envoy to announce the emancipation of all slaves in the South in return for international recognition. Davis consented to put this distasteful proposal before his Cabinet and certain leading Congressmen.

Apart from two or three, like Robert Toombs of Georgia, who strongly approved, those consulted were hostile. Emancipation, they said, would ruin them.

Kenner declared he was asking no one to make a sacrifice which he was not prepared to make himself, and scouted the idea of economic ruin.

In the end and in desperation Davis gave way; he asked Kenner himself to go to Europe as his personal representative, whether the Senate confirmed the appointment or not. Even now Benjamin hesitated: his hesitation may have been due to his prescience that the step was too late or to his reluctance to stultify his previous policy as announced to Slidell and Mason. He was silent and the President acted on his own initiative. Early in 1865, Kenner, partially disguised and facing considerable danger, reached New York and sailed for England. Arrived in London, he obtained an interview with Lord Palmerston who told him that President Davis's proposal could not be entertained without the concurrence of the French Emperor.

> "With the Emperor's concurrence would your Government give us recognition?" enquired Kenner.
>
> "That," was Palmerston's reply, "would be a subject for consideration when the case presents itself and would depend upon circumstances which cannot be foreseen."

From London Kenner proceeded to Paris where he made known his mission to Slidell, with whom he had always been friendly. On his behalf Slidell on March 5, 1865, saw the Emperor and put before him the new proposal about slavery.

Napoleon, according to Slidell, said that he had "never taken this into consideration, that it had not and could not have any influence in his action, but that it had been differently considered in England."

It is true, slavery had never been discussed between them, and it is highly probable that Napoleon had no exaggerated personal antipathy to slavery, but he knew enough of the feelings of the Liberal Opposition and the opinions of many of the leading political and literary figures of the day to recognise the strength of French anti-slavery prejudice.

> "I asked him if he could not renew his overtures to England. He said that they had been so decidedly rejected that he did not suppose that they would now be listened to with more favour.... He is willing and anxious to act with England, but will not move without her.
>
> "We had previously spoken at large of our military situation and I had said that we should soon know whether Beaurégard could effectually check Sherman or whether he was too weak to oppose Sherman's further progress. In either event it would exercise very great influence upon our future movements and policy.... He said that of late the British

Government seemed more disposed to make itself agreeable to him and that he supposed they anticipated trouble from some quarter. It could not well be from any other quarter than the United States.

"I am really at a loss to express any opinion as to the course you should pursue; the situation is embarrassing, as our instructions appear to leave no discretion excepting as to the mode in which we should bring them before the two governments. But they are largely supplemented by the authority given to Mr. Kenner to express the views of the President, and I, were the question still an open one here, would be inclined to follow his suggestions." *

Kenner, recognising that all now depended upon England, carried Napoleon's answer back to Lord Palmerston. But by that time Sherman's army was making its triumphant march through Georgia and Lee was being slowly, but surely, encircled in Virginia.

"It is too late," said Palmerston. It was palpable to the whole world now that the Confederacy was doomed.

A few weeks later and Slidell had abandoned hope.

"We have seen," he wrote Mason (April 26), "the beginning of the end. I, for my part, am

* Slidell to Mason, March 6, 1865.

prepared for the worst. With Lee's surrender there will soon be an end of our regularly organised armies and I can see no possible good to come from a protracted guerilla warfare. We are crushed and must submit to the yoke. Our children must bide their time for vengeance, but you and I will never revisit our homes under our glorious flag. For myself I shall never put my foot on a soil over which flaunts the hated Stars and Stripes.

"I went yesterday to the Foreign Affairs but Mr. C. had already left his office. I have sent Eustis to make the inquiries you desired and shall keep my letter open to give you the result—but before you receive this you will probably have another steamer's news with Lincoln's programme of pacification and reconstruction. I am sick, sick at heart.

"Yours faithfully,
"JOHN SLIDELL."

There is little further to add. The remaining years of Slidell's life do not properly concern these pages. The surrender at Appomattox was followed by the break-up of the Confederacy, the dramatic flight of President Davis and Secretary Benjamin and the end of Slidell's Commissionership in Paris.

Yet although the apartment in the Avenue d'Antin was given up, as well as the office in the rue Marignan, Slidell and his family remained in the French capital with occasional trips to England, until the fall of the Empire. The capture of New Orleans and the confiscation of his property by the Federal authorities long cut off this source of income; yet the property was eventually restored. From afar the aging John Slidell watched the course of events in America.

> "I cannot stomach the word 'pardon,'" he wrote; "no amnesty would be extended to us, certainly neither to Mr. Mason nor to me. Mr. Mann might possibly have some choice of being forgiven, but I have no idea he will make the experiment."

Yet for all that Slidell did apply to President Johnson for permission to return (at least temporarily) to America; but no answer was ever made to his application. Perhaps he expected none.

> "Nothing," he wrote Mason, "would induce me ever to become a citizen of the U.S. nor will any of my children, I trust, ever establish themselves there. Indeed could I return tomorrow to Louisiana, be elected by acclamation to the Senate and received without contradiction at Washington, I would shrink with disgust from any association with those who now pollute the Capitol.
>
> "But having one daughter married in France and Mrs. Slidell with the two others having become not only accustomed to but satisfied with Parisian life— having no interest which could be advanced by my

presence in America—feeling that I could not possibly render any service to any one or any cause at home, I have made up my mind to let the remainder of my days, in the course of nature it cannot be a long one, glide away quietly in Paris. There is no great hardship in this, for there is no spot on earth where the 'dolce far niente' can be more fully enjoyed."

Occasionally, he and his family crossed to England and there Slidell renewed his former intimacy with Judah P. Benjamin, now by an astonishing mutation of fortune, become a prosperous leader of the English bar. There in 1870 Mrs. Slidell, heart-stricken over the ruin of the South, died suddenly. From Benjamin's pen we have a description of her death.

"His family were all at Brighton, when Mrs. Slidell, who was apparently in perfect health (an hour after having left her daughters in good and cheerful spirits in the drawing-room) was found lying senseless on the floor of her bedroom, and she never recovered consciousness."

With the fall of the Empire Slidell left France forever and a few months afterwards, July 2, 1871, he too died at Cowes. Before his death he visited the Emperor Napoleon at Chislehurst; the two exiles shook hands, met each other's gaze steadily, but for some moments could not speak. The memory of the splendid lost chances of the past must have been too potent for utterance.

If—! Too late!—how those twin regrets must have haunted them both!

But as for Judah Philip Benjamin, surnamed the "Brains of the Confederacy," he, serene, rubicund, industrious, went steadily on until, years later, amassing a large fortune, he retired to the beautiful house he had built in Paris, to die.* What a kaleidoscopic career! West Indian Jew, United States Senator, Confederate Secretary of State, English King's Counsel, he became a domiciled Frenchman at the last, the sole truly triumphant survivor of the Lost Cause.

* May 8, 1884. At 43, Avenue d'Iéna. He was survived by his widow and a daughter who was married to Capt. de Bousignac of the French army.